SALES &

OPERATIONS PLANNING

Also by Tom Wallace

Sales Forecasting – A New Approach

ERP: Making It Happen

The Instant Access Guide to World Class Manufacturing

Customer Driven Strategy

The Innovation Edge

High Performance Purchasing

MRP II: Making It Happen

SALES &

OPERATIONS

PLANNING

The "How-To" Handbook

How to Implement It

How to Operate It

How to Use It to Benefit
Your Company, Your Customers,
and Your Supply Chain

Thomas F. Wallace

T. F. Wallace & Company
1999

First Printing: September 1999.
Second Printing: November 1999, minor revisions.
Third Printing: April 2000, minor revisions.
Fourth Printing: July 2000, minor revisions.
Fifth Printing: October 2000
Sixth Printing: January 2001, cover change, revision to address
Seventh Printing: April 2001
Eighth Printing: June 2001, minor revisions
Ninth Printing: November 2001, minor revisions

International Standard Book Number (ISBN): 0-9674884-0-0

Printed in the United States of America

Ten or more copies of this book may be ordered directly from:

T. F. Wallace & Company
453 Stanley Avenue
Cincinnati, Ohio 45226
(513)281-0500/fax: (513)281-0501
E-mail: tomwallace@fuse.net

TABLE OF CONTENTS

Part One — What Is Sales & Operations Planning?

Part Two — How to Make It Work

List of Figures

Dedication

This book is dedicated to the men and women who work in America's manufacturing companies — in jobs that range from the plant floor to the executive suite, in roles that span the gamut from Sales & Marketing to Operations to Product Development to Finance & Accounting to Human Resources.

You have created one of the most remarkable turnarounds in industrial history, from the dark days of the 1970s and 1980s, when we were no longer number one, to where we are now — once again the pre-eminent industrial nation in the world.

You've done an amazing job, and our country owes you a large vote of thanks.

In Appreciation

APICS — The Educational Society for Resource Management has done an excellent job over the years in helping to build the body of knowledge in the field of resource management, and to communicate it broadly. APICS is one of the reasons for the turnaround cited above.

In recognition and appreciation, I have donated a portion of the revenue from the sales of this book to the APICS Education and Research Foundation. I've asked that these donations be used to support the APICS Dictionary, for which I served as editor of the fourth, fifth, and sixth editions.

Acknowledgments

Thanks also go to the talented and highly experienced professionals who reviewed the manuscript of this book and gave invaluable feedback:

Ross Bushman
Vice President, Sales and Planning
Cast-Fab Technologies

Mike Campbell
President and CEO
Demand Management, Inc.

Mike Kremzar
former Vice President, Product Supply Worldwide
The Procter & Gamble Company

Linda LeBlanc
Vice President, Human Resources
Formica Corporation

Dick Ling
President
Richard C. Ling Inc.

Walt Pietrak
North American MRP II Coach
The Procter & Gamble Company

Arvil Sexton
former Vice President, Mfg. Resource Planning
Drexel Heritage Furnishings, Inc.

Bing Sherrill
Vice President, General Manager
Moog Inc. Systems Group

Chandler Stevens
Production Planning
CTL Aerospace

Thanks folks. You made it a lot better.

I owe much gratitude to my partner of 37 years, Evelyn Wallace, who once again displayed great amounts of patience, forbearance, and support during the writing of this, our sixth, book.

Ronn Neff (copy edit), David Mill (cover design), and Tom Brennan (proofing) all did a superb job. For that, I'm not surprised but very grateful. It's a delight to work with real professionals.

Special thanks go to Dick Ling, who is the inventor and prime mover of Sales & Operations Planning. Without Dick's creativity and his drive we wouldn't have this superb tool — and therefore all of us in industry are in Dick's debt.

Last and certainly not least, another special thank you goes to my colleague, Arvil Sexton. Arvil's enthusiasm, dedication, and commitment to helping improve American industry mark him as one of the true leaders in this field. Without him, this book probably wouldn't have been written. Thank you, my friend.

Foreword

Sales & Operations Planning (S&OP) is a superior decision-making process that helps people in companies to provide excellent customer service and to run the business better. It's a great tool, when it's done correctly. However, in my travels, I see too many companies:

- trying to use S&OP but struggling, because they really don't understand it; or,

- trying to implement S&OP but having a hard time, because they really don't understand it; or,

- not considering S&OP, because they really don't understand it.

There's a fair amount of misinformation and mythology about Sales & Operations Planning that's getting in the way. For example ...

Myth: S&OP's just a once-per-month meeting.

Fact: S&OP operates on a monthly cycle, which culminates in the Executive S&OP meeting held around the middle of the month. Prior to that, three important phases take place: Demand Planning, Supply Planning, and the Pre-SOP meeting, where middle management people formulate recommendations for the executive session. All of these earlier activities make it possible for the Executive S&OP meeting to take place two hours or less, thereby making very effective use of top management's time. Sales & Operations Planning is an ongoing, multistep process which occurs every month.

****

Myth: S&OP's no big deal — it's mainly looking at numbers on a spreadsheet.

Fact: The essence of S&OP is decision-making regarding customer service goals, sales volumes, production rates, levels of finished goods inventory, and customer order backlog. The S&OP spreadsheet, one for each major product family, brings all of these elements together into one display. Thus it enables people to view the business holistically — to see the interplay between demand and supply, between customer orders and inventories — and to make solid, informed decisions. Viewing different parts of the business separately can lead people to make suboptimal decisions, as in "the inventories are too high, cut the inventory!" and "our customer service is lousy; we've got to put more into inventories!" An organic, holistic view of the business makes it far easier to avoid such decisions — and to avoid getting into that kind of trouble in the first place.

****

Myth: S&OP deals with product families, so how can it be helpful? You can't learn anything from looking at aggregate numbers.

Fact: We do it all the time. Take investing, for example. When I want to know how the stock market's doing, I check the Dow Jones Industrial Average, the S&P 500, and the Nasdaq. Those three numbers alone give me a good feel for what the market's doing. If they haven't changed a lot from yesterday, last week, last month, then I'm okay and can think about something else. If there's a lot of movement, however, then I may want to get down into the detail and check my individual mutual funds and stocks.

It's similar for a manufacturing enterprise. The picture on aggregate product families shows:

- their levels of customer service;

- how their sales are trending;

- whether production is meeting the overall plan;

- whether the finished inventories and customer order backlogs are where we want them to be, and so on.

With this high-level information, executives and managers can make effective decisions regarding the direction of these important elements of the business. I liken this view of the business to flying in a plane at about 5000 feet off the ground. You can see a lot from up there; you can get the big picture.

Of course, the company has to do more than deal with aggregate volumes. It needs to handle the mix — individual products, customer orders, stockkeeping units. This is the job of tools such as line-item forecasting, customer order promising, master scheduling, and plant and supplier scheduling. Mix is not the big picture; it's the details. Mix is 100 feet off the ground at about 400 knots. I can guarantee you that you can't see the big picture down there.

Incidentally, even though I just used the phrase "manufacturing enterprise," Sales & Operations Planning has application in other environments. For S&OP to be helpful, the output does not have to be a physical product. Organizations such as those involved in design engineering, product development, and computer software can benefit from this process.

****

*Myth: Sales & Operations Planning is just a new term for something that's been around forever —
Production Planning*

Fact: The difference between Sales & Operations Planning and Production Planning is as large as the differences between functional silos and cross-functional teams. The old Production Planning process — the "silo" approach — called for Sales and Marketing to develop the sales forecast and hand it off to Operations for production planning. The resulting production plan was then given to the Master Scheduler to break down into individual products. That's it.

Sales & Operations Planning — a cross-functional process — calls for Sales and Marketing, Operations, Finance, and Product Development to work together to develop an integrated set of plans that all of these departments can support. Then their recommendations are presented to the Executive S&OP Team (another cross-functional group) for their approval or decisions to modify the recommendations. The output of this process is the authorized companywide game plan, far more than a production plan. For more on this topic, see Appendix D.

****

I wrote this book to dispel the myths and to raise awareness of the facts. My hope is that it will help more and more companies take advantage of this powerful decision-making process to help run their businesses better.

Tom Wallace
Cincinnati, Ohio and Bryson City, North Carolina
June 1999

How to Use This Book

This book has two major sections. Part one introduces and describes Sales & Operations Planning, while part two, the larger section, focuses on how to make it work.

Time is money, and typically we don't have enough of either. Not everybody will need to — much less want to — read all of this book. So here are some thoughts as to who might read which chapters, in order to learn what they need to know and still make efficient use of their time.

Companies Operating S&OP

A number of companies today are using Sales & Operations Planning to help manage their businesses, some very successfully. If you're in that category, you probably know quite a bit about S&OP already. Therefore part one of this book, which describes the process, may not add much value for you. However part two, which gets into the details of how to implement it, might help you make improvements. My advice for you folks is to read chapters 6 through 17 (that's all of part two) and double back into part one if you feel the need for clarification.

Many people I talk to in companies using Sales & Operations Planning are curious about how they're doing and how they stack up against other S&OP users. If you're in that category, you might first look at the S&OP Effectiveness Checklist in chapter 16. It should give you a good idea concerning the strong and the not-so-strong aspects of your process and help you prioritize the needed changes.

Companies Implementing S&OP

People in these companies fall into several categories (described in chapter 7):

- Members of the Executive S&OP Team should read at least chapters 1 through 7.

- The Executive Champion and the S&OP Process Owner should read the entire book.

- Anyone who will be "hands-on" with Sales & Operations Planning should read the entire book, including members of the Pre-SOP Team, Demand Planning Team, and Supply Planning Team.

- The senior Information Systems executive should read chapters 9 and 14, in addition to 1 through 7.

- The Spreadsheet Developer should read chapters 1 through 9

Companies Considering S&OP

This book can also be helpful to people in companies that have not yet begun an implementation. Typically they want to know what it is, how it works, why it's important, and how it might help them. They should read chapters 1 through 5. Then, if that's got their interest, they might want to cover the remaining chapters.

Part One

What Is Sales & Operations Planning?

Chapter 1

Sales & Operations Planning Overview

Let's eavesdrop on an executive staff meeting at the Acme Widget Company. The participants are not happy campers.

President: *This shortage situation is terrible. When will we ever get our act together? Whenever business gets good, we run out of product and our customer service is lousy.*

VP Operations: *I'll tell you when. When we start to get some decent forecasts from the Sales Department ...*

VP Sales (interrupting): *Wait a minute. We forecasted this upturn.*

VP Operations: *... in time to do something about it. Yeah, we got the revised forecast — four days after the start of the month. By then it was too late.*

VP Sales: *I could have told you months ago. All you had to do was ask.*

VP Finance: *I'd like to be in on those conversations. We've been burned more than once by building inventories for a business upturn that doesn't happen. Then we get stuck with tons of inventory and run out of cash.*

And the beat goes on. Back orders, dissatisfied customers, high inventories, late shipments, finger-pointing, cash-flow problems, demand and supply out of balance, missing the business plan. This is the norm in many companies.

It does not, however, have to be that way. Today many companies are using a business process called Sales & Operations Planning (S&OP) to help avoid such problems. To learn what it is, and how to make it work, read on.

What Is Sales & Operations Planning?

How would you like a process to help you give better customer service, lower your inventories, shorten customer lead times, stabilize production rates, give top management a real handle on the business, and build teamwork between Sales, Operations, Finance, and Product Development?

Such a process exists. Would you like this tool to be relatively easy to implement, not cost much, and start to generate results within a few months of getting started? It's all of those things. It's called Sales & Operations Planning (S&OP), and a growing number of companies are using it to sharply improve their ability to run the business. It helps them to get demand and supply in balance, *and to keep them in balance*. Balancing demand and supply is essential to running a business well, and this balancing must occur at both the aggregate, volume level and at the detailed, mix level.

We've just identified four fundamentals: demand and supply, volume and mix. Let's look at the first pair.

Demand and Supply

What happens when demand and supply aren't in balance? Well, if demand greatly exceeds supply (see the scale below), bad things happen:

- Customer service suffers. The company can't ship product to its customers when they want it. Customer lead times stretch out as the order backlog builds. Business is lost as customers go elsewhere.

- Costs increase. Unplanned overtime goes up. Premium freight rises. Purchase price variances become unfavorable.

- Quality often "gets lost in the shuffle" as the company strives mightily to get product shipped. Specifications get compromised or waived. Temporary subcontracting yields a less robust product. Material from alternate suppliers often doesn't process as well.

Isn't this great? Owing to demand exceeding supply, performance deteriorates on three fundamental attributes: cost, quality, and delivery. Business is lost, costs go up, and thus the bottom line takes a hit. Similarly, when supply substantially exceeds demand, bad things happen:

- Inventories increase, carrying costs rise, and cash flow can become a problem.

- Production rates are cut. Volume variances turn unfavorable. Layoffs are

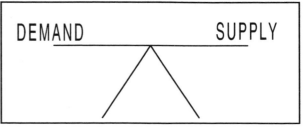

a possibility and morale suffers. People in the plant slow down and efficiency numbers start to drop.

- Profit margins get squeezed. Prices are cut. Discounting increases. Deals and promotions become more frequent.

Well, that's not good either. Supply exceeds demand and the company is stuck with lower margins, higher costs, a cash crunch, and the possibility of layoffs.

Now, is it always bad if demand and supply aren't in balance? No, sometimes it can be a good thing. It all depends on where the imbalance lies. For example, if projected demand ten months in the future exceeds current supply, and if the company can economically add more capacity sooner than that, that's fine. Demand is growing; business is good. Being able to see the projected imbalances soon enough is what's needed.

The name of the game therefore is to get demand and supply *in balance* and to keep them there. It's that simple. Balance demand and supply. Have processes in place to do it. Have early warning capabilities to alert people that they're getting out of sync. Make the corrections early — surgically — so that they can be small, as opposed to making large, radical corrections later with a meat cleaver.

Volume and Mix

The other two fundamentals are volume and mix. As with demand and supply, we need to treat them separately in our thinking. If volume is handled effectively, it's much less difficult to deal with mix problems as they arise. On the other hand, if volume is not planned well, then mix issues become substantially more difficult to cope with. Many companies get themselves in trouble because they can't distinguish volume-related problems from those of mix. In the box on the next page, we can see the difference between the two: volume is the big picture, and mix is the details.

Questions of volume precede those of mix, so smart companies plan their volumes first, and spend enough time and effort to do it well. They find that doing so makes mix problems much less difficult. But where do most companies spend almost all of their time? On mix. Many look at volumes only once per year, when they do the Business Plan. They probably wouldn't do it even that often, except the financial folks make them do it. They have to set production rates in order to nail down overhead absorption, which of course is necessary to cost the products.

Volume versus Mix		
Volume	=	The Big Picture: How Much? Rates Product Families
Mix	=	The Details: Which ones? Sequence Individual products and customer orders

Why is that? Why do most companies spend more than 99 percent of their time on mix issues to the exclusion of volume? It's simple: mix — individual products — is what companies ship to their customers. That's where the pressure is. Mix is seen as important and urgent. The effective planning of future volumes may be seen as important, but it carries less urgency.

As a result, many companies set their volumes — sales rates and production rates — no more than once per year. But how often during an average year do volume needs change? It's almost always more often than once every twelve months. For most companies, it's more than once per quarter.

I submit that most companies don't work hard enough at forecasting and planning their volumes and spend too much time trying to predict mix. They overwork the details and don't focus enough on the big picture.

Back to the four fundamentals: demand and supply, volume and mix. Shipping product to customers with world-class reliability and speed requires that all four of these elements be well managed and controlled.

S&OP's mission is to balance demand and supply at the *volume* level. Volume refers to rates — overall rates of sales, rates of production, aggregate inventories, and order backlogs. Companies have found that when they do a good job of planning and replanning volume — rates and levels — as they go through the year, then problems with *mix* — individual products and orders — become less difficult to deal with. Companies have found they can ship better, ship more quickly, and do it with less inventory.

For those of you who like formal definitions, I offer this:

> Sales & Operations Planning (S&OP) is a business process that helps companies keep **demand and supply in balance.** It does that by focusing on **aggregate volumes** — product families and groups — so that mix issues — individual products and customer orders — can be handled more readily. It occurs on a **monthly** cycle and displays information in both **units and dollars.** S&OP is **cross-functional**, involving General Management, Sales, Operations, Finance, and Product Development. It occurs at **multiple levels** within the company, up to and **including the executive in charge of the business unit,** e.g. division president, business unit general manager, or CEO of a smaller corporation. S&OP **links the company's Strategic Plans and Business Plan to its detailed processes** — the order entry, master scheduling, plant scheduling, and purchasing tools it uses to run the business on a week-to-week, day-to-day, and hour-to-hour basis. Used properly, S&OP enables the company's managers to view the business **holistically** and gives them a **window into the future.**

What Are the Benefits?

Benefits resulting from effective Sales & Operations Planning include:

- For make-to-stock companies: higher customer service and often lower finished goods inventories — *at the same time.*

- For make-to-order companies: higher customer service, and often shorter customer lead times — *at the same time.*

- More stable production rates and less overtime, leading to higher productivity.

- Enhanced teamwork among the middle-management people from Sales, Operations, Finance, and Product Development.*

---

*Throughout this handbook, I use the term "Sales" to refer to all of the sales and marketing functions throughout the company, i.e. the demand side of the business. "Operations" refers to the manufacturing, materials, and logistics functions, i.e. the supply-side activities.

- Enhanced teamwork among the executive group.

- Greater accountability regarding actual performance to plan.

- A monthly update to the Business Plan, leading to better forward visibility and fewer surprises late in the fiscal year.

- The ability to make changes *quickly* off a common game plan.

- Last and certainly not least, S&OP provides a "window into the future." It's uncanny, but the process — when done well — truly does enable people to better see what's coming at them. S&OP enhances pro-active decision-making.

Executives who've implemented S&OP swear by it. Let's hear from some:

- *Sales & Operations Planning addresses the very same issues that are vital to our customers — what they need and how we're going to get it to them.* — Vice President, Sales

- *Because we're looking ahead every month, we're able to make production rate changes sooner and at times spread the impact. This means these changes are easier for us and our work force to respond to. And they cost less.* — Vice President, Operations

- *The benefits from Sales & Operations Planning have been significant and continue to grow. Some of our business units have experienced a 20 percent improvement in customer service levels while costs have decreased.* — Vice President, Product Supply

- *In some of our make-to-order businesses, as a direct result of S&OP we've reduced lead times to customers by up to 50 percent.* — Vice President/Group General Manager

Perhaps the best testimonial of all came from the head of the North American component of a UK-based multinational. At the conclusion of an S&OP meeting where some very difficult decisions were made, he turned to me and said:

> *Tom, when I think back to a year ago, before we had S&OP, I wonder how we were able to run the business without it. — Division Chief Executive*

Sales & Operations Planning really is top management's handle on the business.

Why Is Top Management Necessary?

Saying it another way, does the boss really need to be involved, and if so, why? Well, I believe that active, involved leadership and participation by the head of the business unit is essential for S&OP to work anywhere near its full potential. The two most important reasons are stewardship and leadership.

Many of the decisions made in S&OP affect the Financial Plan for the current year, and top management "owns" that Business Plan. They have a stewardship responsibility for it, and only they can make decisions to change it. When the Business Plan is not changed to reflect the new Sales & Operations Plan, there's a disconnect between the financial numbers top management is expecting to be achieved and the forecasts and production plans being used to operate the business. "Best in class" performance in this area means that the business is managed — at all levels — using one and only one set of numbers.

Participation by the heads of the business makes a strong leadership statement that S&OP is the process being used to manage these highly important activities: integrating operational and financial planning, balancing demand and supply, and enhancing customer service. This "encourages" other people throughout the organization to do their part in supporting the process. Without such leadership by senior management, participation in the S&OP process is often viewed as optional, with the result that over time the process erodes and then goes away.

Executive participation shouldn't be a problem, because so relatively little of their time is required. We're talking about one meeting per month, lasting for two hours or less. This event, called the Executive Sales & Operations Planning meeting, can often replace several other meetings and thus result in a net reduction in meeting time. For presidents, preparation time is zero. For members of their staff, some preparation time may be helpful — mainly in the form of briefings by their people — to enable the necessary sign-offs to take place.

So how can something so productive require so little time? Well, most of the heavy lifting is done in earlier steps in the process: middle-management people update the forecast, aggregate the data into product family groupings, identify capacity constraints and raw material problems, and formulate the recommendations to be presented in the top management meeting.

Where Does It Fit?

At this point, it may be helpful to look at Figure 1-1 on the next page, which depicts the structure of the resource planning process. Starting from the top, you can probably tell that I don't much care if you call it Manufacturing Resource Planning (MRP II), Business Resource Planning (BRP), or Enterprise Resource Planning (ERP). For our purposes here, the differences among these three are not significant.** Several points in Figure 1-1 are worthy of our attention:

- The horizontal dotted line indicates that Strategic Planning and Business Planning are not integral parts of the overall resource planning process. Rather, they are important drivers into the process.

- Sales & Operations Planning forms an essential *linkage,* tying the Strategic and Business Plans together with the Master Scheduling function. It's the Master Schedule that serves as the source of customer order promising and drives all of the "downstream" schedules for the plants and the suppliers.

In companies without S&OP, there is frequently a disconnect between the Business Plan and the Master Schedule. In other words, the plans that top management has helped to develop and has authorized are not connected to the plans and schedules that drive day-to-day activities on the plant floor, the receiving dock, and most important, the shipping dock. That is why some companies frequently get "surprises" late in the fiscal year.

How Does S&OP Support Supply Chain Management?

I think S&OP does more than support Supply Chain Management; I believe it's an integral part of it. A given supply chain probably won't work well if its various members don't have good volume plans in the first place and if they're slow to react to the inevitable changes in volume. Sales &

**For readers new to this field, I should point out that the terminology here leaves a bit to be desired. MRP II and BRP can be considered as synonymous, and the differences between these two and ERP are essentially in the software: ERP software is more robust and is better able to integrate operations within diverse business units. At the heart of all of them are the *business processes* to balance demand and supply, provide superior customer service, and manage the resources of the business well.

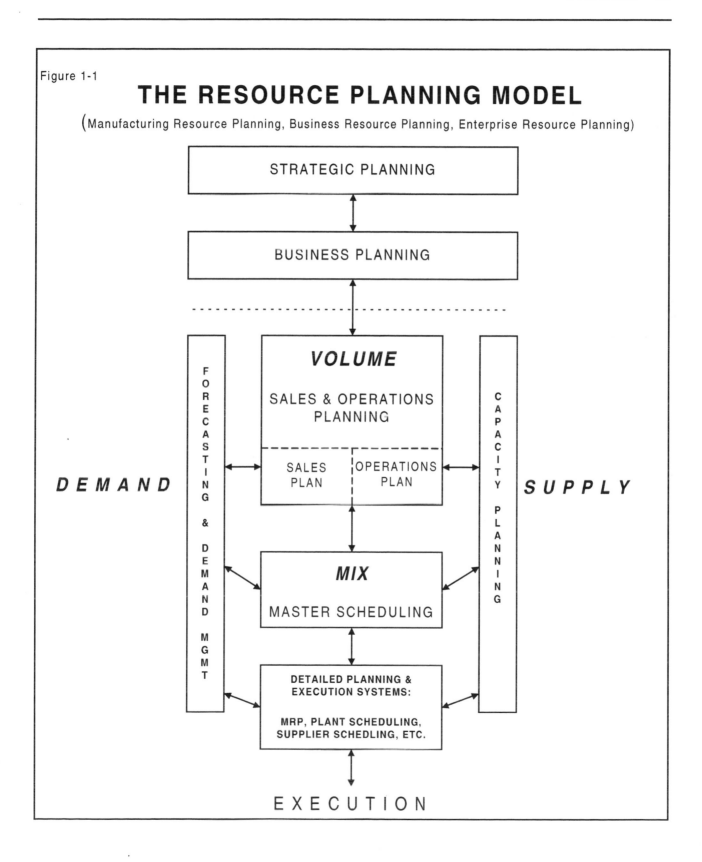

Figure 1-1

THE RESOURCE PLANNING MODEL

(Manufacturing Resource Planning, Business Resource Planning, Enterprise Resource Planning)

Operations Planning can be considered as a *lubricant* between partners in the supply chain, enabling the total chain to function harmoniously and with minimum disruption.

Supply chains extend in two directions: forward to the customers and backward to suppliers. Regarding customer service, we've already seen examples and heard testimonials from executives on S&OP's contribution to improved customer service performance. And I believe this is the biggest supply chain benefit of all: *S&OP will help you provide superior customer service.*

Regarding backward in the supply chain, toward the suppliers, S&OP's contribution there is also significant. The benefits can be much the same for suppliers as for a company's internal production processes. Provided the company shares its S&OP results with key suppliers, then these suppliers should experience:

* more stable production rates,

* volume changes made sooner and smaller, and hence more economically — rather than later and larger, and thus more expensively,

* a greater ability to respond to mix changes, because the volume picture is under control.

Supplier partnering calls for shared information and plans. This is based on the premise that the more advance notice you can give suppliers, the better they will be able to support your needs. Very simply, S&OP provides the future volume plans for suppliers — off the same common plan that top management has authorized for internal production.

Procter & Gamble does a superb job of managing its supply chains; it's one of the best in the world at that. Mike Kremzar, who served as Vice President, Product Supply Worldwide during that company's drive to supply chain excellence, sums it up: "With an effective S&OP process, the supply chain can be optimized to become a true competitive advantage with costs, speed, and inventories at levels thought to be unreachable."

How Much Does It Cost?

Surprisingly little. Since it involves relatively few people — dozens, not hundreds, in an average-sized business — the education and training costs are low. It normally doesn't require a full-time project team or even, frequently, a full-time project leader. Software plays a relatively minor role in Sales & Operations Planning, so computer costs range from moderate to zero.

Regarding the latter point, many companies have found that S&OP will require them to do a more rigorous job of forecasting and that good forecasting software will help them do that. I've seen companies spend less than $50,000 for a fine, effective, user-friendly forecasting package. For the S&OP spreadsheet itself, most companies use spreadsheet software from Excel, Quattro-Pro, or Lotus 1-2-3. They all work fine. We're starting to see the onset of commercially available S&OP software packages; one that I'm familiar with has a price tag of less than $25,000.

The other expenditure that some companies incur is consulting costs. We'll discuss this aspect of implementation in chapter 7, but for now let's just point out that these costs are typically around $50,000 over the life of the six- to ten-month implementation cycle.

To sum up, if you decide to buy forecasting and S&OP software and to use a consultant, the project will cost around $125,000 out of pocket. If you don't need software and decide not to use a consultant, your out-of-pocket costs will be near zero.

Some experienced S&OP users claim that the benefits from Sales & Operations Planning equal or exceed those from their ERP system. S&OP typically costs less than $100,000; installing an ERP software system normally costs millions of dollars.

FREQUENTLY ASKED QUESTIONS

We don't have a full-blown resource planning system (ERP/MRP II) in our company. Does that mean we can't use Sales & Operations Planning?

Not at all. Even though S&OP was developed as an integral part of MRP II/ERP, it's been proven to work very well on a stand-alone basis. My advice: don't delay S&OP waiting for the implementation of a full-blown resource planning system. Get started now so you can start to get the benefits from S&OP. Then, when you do implement a resource planning system, it'll work much better because you'll have demand and supply balanced at the volume level.

Keep in mind that most ERP systems deal almost entirely with issues of *mix*, not volume. One reason many companies have been bitterly disappointed with the results from their massive investments in ERP software is, quite simply, they haven't implemented Sales & Operations Planning. Why not? Frequently it's because no S&OP module came with their ERP software package. As a result it's not on the radar screen of the project team and system integrators. And thus it doesn't get done.

The result is that the company is left with software, and sometimes better processes, to help manage the mix — but *volume* is being addressed formally only once per year. So if this scenario describes your company, consider that S&OP could give you the opportunity to help make your ERP invest-mended really pay off.

****

Sales & Operations Planning sounds pretty formal. Is it too rigid?

Dick Ling says it very well: "S&OP's all about managing change." Think about it: if things never changed, or changed only once per year, there would be no need for S&OP. It's there because things change.

Sales & Operations Planning gives you the ability to make changes very quickly, because there's an agreed-upon game plan already in place. Without S&OP, there's seldom a total plan; each department has its own. With S&OP, the foundation's already there because the key players have already bought into one single plan. All that needs to be addressed are the deltas arising from new conditions.

Chapter 2

The Structure and Logic of
Sales & Operations Planning

What follows is an example from a fictitious manufacturer of widgets for home and industry. This company is not yet using Sales & Operations Planning.

Bad Day at Acme Widget

Mike Marshall, a product manager at Acme Widget, is doing his quarterly review of the forecasts for his products. He's looking at a summary spreadsheet for the Medium Consumer Widget product family.

	FEB	MAR	APR	MAY	JUN	JUL	AUG	SEP
FORECAST (in 000 units)	100	100	100	100	120	120	120	120
ACTUAL SALES	90	95	85					
DIFFERENCE	−10	−5	−15					
CUM DIFFERENCE		−15	−30					

Mike is concerned that actual sales are consistently below forecast. Over the last three months, actual sales have been 10 percent below forecast. Mike scratches his head, checks a couple of reports he recently received from field sales people, and concludes that this product family is losing business to another family that the company introduced recently. He decides to revise the forecast downward and, with a few quick strokes on his computer keyboard, does so.

	FEB	MAR	APR		MAY	JUN	JUL	AUG	SEP
FORECAST (in 000 units)	100	100	100	OLD FORECAST	100	120	120	120	120
				NEW FORECAST	90	90	90	90	90
ACTUAL SALES	90	95	85						
DIFFERENCE	−10	−5	−15						
CUM DIFFERENCE		−15	−30						

Mike has reduced his forecast by 10,000 per month in May and by 30,000 per month after that, thereby wiping out the forecast increase that he had made for June and beyond. Remembering a conversation he had recently with Carol Clark, the chief financial officer, about high inventories, he decides to notify the plant of the forecast change. He sends Pete Prentis, the plant manager, an e-mail, containing the spreadsheet shown above.

Pete reacts to the e-mail message by checking his production plan for Medium Consumer Widgets:

	FEB	MAR	APR	MAY	JUN	JUL	AUG	SEP
PLANNED PRODUCTION (in 000 units)	100	100	100	110	120	120	120	120
ACTUAL PRODUCTION	98	100	101					
DIFFERENCE	–2	—	+1					
CUM DIFFERENCE	–2	–2	–1					

Pete scratches his head and thinks to himself, *Man, this is a double whammy. Not only is he dropping the forecast, he's taking out the increase set for June. And we're already ramping up to 120,000 per month. Nuts!* Pete calls Mike; they talk a bit, and Pete concludes there's no choice but to cut production back. He lays out a new plan, recognizing that there's not much he can do to cut back the May output, since the month is already more than half over:

	FEB	MAR	APR		MAY	JUN	JUL	AUG	SEP
PLANNED PRODUCTION	100	100	100	OLD PLAN	110	120	120	120	120
				NEW PLAN	110	100	100	90	90
ACTUAL PRODUCTION	98	100	101						
DIFFERENCE	–2	—	+1						
CUM DIFFERENCE		–2	–1						

Meanwhile, back in the Finance department, Carol the CFO has just finished a rather difficult phone call with the company's banker. It centered on such things as excess inventories, negative cash flow, and the need to increase the line of credit. Carol promised the banker that she personally would dig into these problems and get them fixed.

She takes a look at her finished goods inventory report and soon comes across the page for Medium Consumer Widgets:

	FEB	MAR	APR	MAY	JUN	JUL	AUG	SEP
PLANNED INVENTORY (1-MO SUPPLY)	100	100	100	110	120	120	120	120
ACTUAL INVENTORY	103	111	116	132				
DIFFERENCE	+3	+11	+16	+32				

Carol's concerned about the inventory build-up on Medium Consumer Widgets. They now have 132,000 units in stock, which is much higher than the budgeted one-month supply. At a standard cost of $50 each, that's $1,600,000 over plan. She calls Pete at the plant: *Pete, the inventory of Medium Widgets is way up there — 30 percent above authorized. Are you guys working on bringing that down? If so, can I count on the inventory starting to drop?*

Pete replies, *Carol, we're aware of the problem. The bad news is that it's a lot worse than your numbers are showing.* He tells her about Mike's downward forecast revision, and they arrange to meet that afternoon. Later, at their meeting, Pete shows Carol Mike's new forecast and his new production plan.

Mike's Forecast:

	FEB	MAR	APR		MAY	JUN	JUL	AUG	SEP
FORECAST	100	100	100	NEW FORECAST	90	90	90	90	90
ACTUAL SALES	90	95	85						
DIFFERENCE	−10	−5	−15						
CUM DIFFERENCE		−15	−30						

Pete's Production Plan:

	FEB	MAR	APR		MAY	JUN	JUL	AUG	SEP
PLANNED PRODUCTION	100	100	100	NEW PLAN	110	100	100	90	90
ACTUAL PRODUCTION	98	100	101						
DIFFERENCE	−2	—	+1						
CUM DIFFERENCE		−2	−1						

Carol, fearing the worst, picks up a pencil and calculates the projected inventory out into the future. She does this by starting with the 132 finished inventory balance at the end of April, subtracting the sales forecast for each month, and adding in Pete's planned production. Here's what she comes up with:

	APR	*MAY*	*JUN*	*JUL*	*AUG*	*SEP*
INV.	*132*	*152*	*162*	*172*	*172*	*172*

Good grief! is Carol's response. *This is awful. The inventory's going over 170,000 — and staying there! That's almost twice as much as we need. At $50 each, we're going to have $8½ million tied up in Medium Widgets. Our budget for all finished goods is $10 million. What's going on here?*

Hey, don't blame me, counters Pete. *I just got the new forecast this morning. Seems to me they should have called those numbers down months ago. I've been saying for a long time that Sales doesn't look at the forecasts often enough.*

Carol: *Pete, I'm afraid you'll need to cut production back a lot more than what you've got here. We just can't live with that inventory.*

Pete: *Well, if we gotta then we gotta. But that means a layoff, which not only costs money but will really drag down morale. And when morale goes down, so does productivity.*

Carol: *I'll get this on the agenda for Monday's executive staff meeting and we can present the issue then. In the meantime, I'll touch base with Mike to see if maybe they can do something to jack up sales.*

What's Wrong with This Picture?

A lot. Let's give some constructive criticism to Mike, Pete, and Carol:

- Mike's not reviewing his forecasts frequently enough. A once-per-quarter review simply isn't adequate for most businesses; they're too fast-paced, too dynamic, and too subject to change.

- As a result, demand and supply have become way out of balance. Pete, the plant manager, is faced with a severe cutback in output rates and a likely layoff.

- The activities are disconnected. Each person is looking at his or her part of the business, but nowhere is the entire picture being brought together. The CFO, Carol, is in this particular loop only because the bank has been hassling her.

- The problem is sufficiently serious that Carol will escalate it to the executive staff meeting. This will most likely consume a fair amount of time, be a difficult discussion, and include some finger-pointing and fault-finding. It will not tend to enhance teamwork among the top management team.

Bottom line: they lack a process to routinely review the status of demand and supply, and to make timely informed decisions about keeping them in balance. What's lacking at Acme Widget is a process like Sales & Operations Planning.

A Better Way to Look at It

Let's pretend for a moment that Acme was just beginning to implement S&OP. Sally Smith, the sales administration manager, is heading up the implementation project and she has just put together an S&OP spreadsheet for Medium Consumer Widgets, a make-to-stock product family. Here's what it might look like.

	FEB	MAR	APR	MAY	JUN	JUL	AUG	SEP
FORECAST	100	100	100	100	120	120	120	120
ACTUAL SALES	90	95	85					
DIFFERENCE	−10	−5	−15					
CUM DIFFERENCE		−15	−30					
PLANNED PRODUCTION	100	100	100	110	120	120	120	120
ACTUAL PRODUCTION	98	100	101					
DIFFERENCE	−2	—	+1					
CUM DIFF		−2	−1					
PLANNED INVENTORY								
(1-MO SUPPLY)	100	100	100	142	142	142	142	142
ACTUAL INV (JAN=103)	111	116	132					
DIFFERENCE	+11	+16	+32					

Let's examine this display for a moment. Notice how both the demand and supply pictures are shown adjacent to each other. They're followed by the inventory projection, which in effect is the critique of the demand/supply relationship.

The benefit is a holistic picture of the status of the product family. This kind of display contains information specific to each of the three key functions: forecasts and actual sales performance for Sales, the production plan and performance to it for Operations, and the inventory status and outlook for the people in Finance, among others.

Each function can view not only its own numbers but also those from other areas. That makes it much easier for managers from a variety of functions to view the business as an organic whole, rather than looking only at their part of it. In the example above, we can see the inventory growth far above plan. We can also track back to the cause: actual sales below forecast. If Sally Smith and her colleagues at Acme Widget had been looking at these numbers every month, they would have been able to *take action sooner* — and not have had to deal with such a major problem as the one they're now facing.

One of the early users of Sales & Operations Planning was the U.S. Pharmaceutical Division of Abbott Labs. Its president stated, *Marketing can challenge Production proposals, Finance can question advertising concepts, and all disciplines participate in the finalization of the [production rate] proposed by Materials Management. My goal is to get everyone seeing the business through my glasses.*[*]

S&OP is a monthly process that involves both middle management and the executive group. It's done in aggregate groupings (families, categories), not in detail. For each of a half-dozen to a dozen major product families, the process focuses on a review of:

- **Recent past performance.** It compares actual performance against plan for sales, production, customer service (on-time shipments), inventory or customer order backlog — and highlights the deviations. This visibility into past performance enhances accountability, and that can be a major benefit. The future plans represent commitments by Sales and by Operations; the actual numbers show how well they did in hitting those plans. In a number of companies, I've seen this fact alone help reduce the gap between plan and actual performance.

- **The outlook for the future.** New, updated Sales Forecasts and the resulting Operations Plans (production plans) are developed, modified where necessary, and authorized. (The Operations Plan is the Sales Forecast plus or minus changes in inventories or backlog to meet the customer service targets, seasonal requirements, plant shutdowns, etc.)

The Make-to-Stock View

An important aspect of S&OP is the ability to focus on customer service and its interplay with inventories (or customer order backlogs for a purely make-to-order business). See Figure 2-1, which is a slightly simplified example of an S&OP spreadsheet. This spreadsheet shows the three prior months' sales and production performance, the finished goods inventory, and the customer service levels achieved. We can see that sales have exceeded forecast by 44,000 units, and this has reduced the finished goods inventories to an unacceptably low level. Why unacceptably low? Because customer service is plummeting. It's nowhere near the target of 99 percent. The forward decisions

---

*"Game Planning," by David Rucinski. *Production and Inventory Management Journal,* First Quarter 1982, pp 63-68.

Figure 2-1   THE ACME WIDGET COMPANY -- SALES & OPERATIONS PLAN FOR OCT 1999

FAMILY: MEDIUM WIDGETS (MAKE-TO-STOCK)   UNIT OF MEASURE: 1000 UNITS

TARGET LINE FILL: 99%   TARGET FIN INV: 10 DAYS ON HAND

| | HISTORY | | | | | | | | | 3rd | 4th | NEXT 12 | FISCAL YEAR | BUSINESS |
SALES	J	A	S	O	N	D	J	F	M	3 MOS	3 MOS	MOS	LATEST CALL	PLAN
NEW FORECAST	200	200	200	210	210	220	220	220	220	690	690	2670	$25,540	$25,400
ACTUAL SALES	222	195	227											
DIFF: MONTH	22	-5	27											
CUM		17	44											

OPERATIONS

	J	A	S	O	N	D	J	F	M	3rd 3 MOS	4th 3 MOS	NEXT 12 MOS		
NEW PLAN	200	200	200	210	220	230	230	230	230	695	690	2735		
ACTUAL	200	206	199											
DIFF: MONTH	0	6	-1											
CUM		6	5											

INVENTORY

	J	A	S	O	N	D	J	F	M	3rd 3 MOS	4th 3 MOS			
PLAN	100	100	100	60	70	80	90	100	110	115	115			
ACTUAL	78	89	61											
DAYS ON HAND	8	9	6	6	6	7	8	9	10	10	9			
LINE FILL %	97%	98%	89%											

DEMAND ISSUES AND ASSUMPTIONS   SUPPLY ISSUES

1. FORECAST RELECTS LAUNCH OF NEW   1. XMAS FULL PLANT SHUTDOWN RESCHEDULED TO
   DESIGNER WIDGET LINE IN 3RD QTR.   STAGGERED PARTIALS THRU FALL AND WINTER
2. ASIA FORECASTED TO REACH 1996 VOLUME

will then focus on:

- the possibility of an increase to the Sales Forecast,

- how quickly production can gear up to get the inventories back to their target level, and

- what actions can be taken in the short run to minimize the negative impacts of the sub-par customer service levels.

One of the important things we've learned from Total Quality Management is that facts arc our friends. Sales & Operations Planning gets all of the relevant facts on one sheet of paper. This helps to avoid suboptimal decisions, where one aspect of the business is improved at a disproportionate cost to another. For example, decisions are sometimes made by looking solely at inventory levels, and the outcome is a mandate to cut production in order to get the inventories down. Several months later the customer service statistics show a horrible performance, so the word goes out to crank up production so we can start to ship on time. And on and on.

S&OP avoids this by displaying planned and actual data for sales, production, inventories, and most important, customer service — all on the same page. In my experience, executives find this very helpful, because it helps them make better decisions.

The Make-to-Order View

Figure 2-2   THE ACME WIDGET COMPANY -- SALES & OPERATIONS PLAN FOR OCT 1999

FAMILY: LARGE WIDGETS (MAKE-TO-ORDER)   UNIT OF MEASURE: EACH

TARGET LINE FILL: 99%   TARGET ORDER BACKLOG: 6 WEEKS

BOOKINGS	J	A	S	O	N	D	J	F	M	3rd 3 MOS	4th 3 MOS	NEXT 12 MOS	FISC YEAR LATEST CALL	BUSINESS PLAN
		HISTORY												
NEW FORECAST	20	20	20	20	20	20	20	20	20	60	60	240	$1,800M	$1,800M
ACTUAL BOOKINGS	22	20	21	20	10	4								
DIFF: MONTH	2	0	1											
CUM		2	3											

PRODUCTION/SHIPMENTS	J	A	S	O	N	D	J	F	M	3rd 3 MOS	4th 3 MOS
NEW PLAN	20	20	20	20	20	20	20	20	20	60	60
ACTUAL	20	21	20								
DIFF: MONTH	0	1	0								
CUM		1	1								

ORDER BACKLOG	J	A	S	O	N	D	J	F	M	3rd 3 MOS	4th 3 MOS
PLAN		30	30	30	30	30	30	30	30	30	30
ACTUAL	28	30	29	30							
WEEKS OF BACKLOG	6	6	6	6	6	6	6	6	6	6	6
ORDER FILL %	99%	100%	100%								

DEMAND ISSUES AND ASSUMPTIONS   SUPPLY ISSUES

1. FORECAST ASSUMES NO CHANGES IN
     COMPETITOR PRICING OR BACKLOG.

The logic of Sales & Operations Planning for make-to-order products is *almost* identical to make-to-stock. The big difference, as shown in Figure 2-2, is that the finished goods inventory is no longer in the picture but is replaced by the customer order backlog.

"Backlog" refers to all customer orders received but not yet shipped, regardless of when they're due to ship. It's actually "negative inventory." Finished goods inventory is what has been produced ahead of receiving customer orders for it. Backlog represents orders received ahead of producing the products.

The size of the customer order backlog is an important competitive factor. The backlog is a primary determiner of lead time to customers because the bigger the backlog, the longer the lead time. If the backlog gets too big and hence the lead times get too long, then the customers might not want to wait. They may go somewhere else where they can get the product sooner. If the backlog gets too small, Operations and possibly other departments can have problems; there may not be enough work to stay efficient. Sales & Operations Planning helps make-to-order manufacturers manage the size of their customer order backlogs; thanks to S&OP's superior visibility, it's easier to keep those backlogs where they should be.

Here's an example. Let's imagine that Acme Widget salespeople see an opportunity in the marketplace: if they could cut their lead times from six weeks to four, they feel they would capture business from the competition. Operations agrees that this is practical and lays out a plan to cut the backlog by two weeks. The resulting plan, which could easily become a formal recommendation to the executive group, might look like Figure 2-3. Operations is committing to a temporary 15 percent ramp-up in production, from 20 units per month to 23. They could possibly ramp up higher and thus reach the four-week backlog target sooner, but as the supply comment points out, this plan is conservative and cost-effective. Starting in March, the plan is to drop back to 21 and then 20. Of course the hope is that the new four-week customer lead time will get more business and thus Acme might not have to drop back from 23 to 20 per month.

We'll return to this issue of the S&OP spreadsheet in chapter 9, when we'll get into the nitty-gritty of spreadsheet design, formulas, and enhancements to what we've seen here.

Figure 2-3   THE ACME WIDGET COMPANY – SALES & OPERATIONS PLAN FOR OCT 1999

FAMILY: LARGE WIDGETS (MAKE-TO-ORDER)   UNIT OF MEASURE: EACH

TARGET LINE FILL: 99%   **TARGET ORDER BACKLOG: 4 WEEKS**

BOOKINGS	HISTORY			O	N	D	J	F	M	3rd 3 MOS	4th 3 MOS	NEXT 12 MOS	FISC YR LATEST CALL	BUSINESS PLAN
	J	A	S											
NEW FORECAST	20	20	20	20	20	20	20	20	20	60	60	240	$1,800M	$1,800M
ACTUAL BOOKINGS	22	20	21	20	10	4								
DIFF: MONTH	2	0	1											
CUM		2	3											

PRODUCTION/SHIPMENTS												
OLD PLAN	20	20	20	20	20	20	20	20	20	60	60	
NEW PLAN				20	21	22	23	23	21	60	60	
ACTUAL	20	21	20									
DIFF: MONTH	0	1	0									
CUM		1	1									

ORDER BACKLOG												
OLD PLAN		30	30	30	30	30	30	30	30	30	30	30
NEW PLAN					30	29	27	24	21	20	20	20
ACTUAL	28	30	29	30								
BACKLOG – # WEEKS					6	6	5	5	4	4		
ORDER FILL %		99%	100%	100%								

DEMAND ISSUES AND ASSUMPTIONS   SUPPLY ISSUES

1. FORECAST ASSUMES NO CHANGES IN   1. PRODUCTION RAMP-UP TO REACH 4-WK BACKLOG IS CONSERVATIVE
       COMPETITOR PRICING OR BACKLOG.   BUT COST-EFFECTIVE.

2. FORECAST DOES NOT RELECT INCREASED
       SALES DUE TO SHORTER BACKLOG.

FREQUENTLY ASKED QUESTIONS

Why does the make-to-stock spreadsheet show finished goods inventory only? What about raw materials and work in process (WIP)?

Several reasons, one being that they're not an integral part of the S&OP logic, which focuses on the interplay between demand, supply, and the level of finished goods. There are other tools available to manage raw material and WIP inventories: Master Scheduling, MRP, and Plant and Supplier Scheduling. These processes take their marching orders from S&OP, which of course is focusing on demand and supply for products.

Another reason is that often it's impossible to tie the raw-material inventory to specific product families. On the other hand, if you can segregate the data validly, there's nothing wrong with displaying raw material and WIP numbers on the spreadsheet as memo entries — provided it would add value and not just clutter.

Chapter 3

Inputs to S&OP

The two major inputs to Sales & Operations Planning are, quite simply, demand and supply. That figures, because S&OP's job is to help people get demand and supply in balance — and to keep them in balance.

Demand Input: Sales Forecasting

In some companies, the toughest part of implementing Sales & Operations Planning is overcoming a deep reluctance to forecast. Let's look at five fundamental questions that surround this problem.

Why Bother with Forecasting?

It's amazing, but I still hear this question from time to time. Often it comes from the same people who say, "You can't forecast this business."

My response is Nuts. Of course the business can be forecasted — perhaps not with great precision, but it certainly can be done. As a matter of fact, virtually all businesses do a significant degree of forecasting. (The only ones who don't are those whose order fulfillment time to their customers is *longer* than their total lead time to get material and capacity. Have you seen many of those lately?)

The problem in many companies is that people in Operations do the "forecasting" by default, i.e. they order the long-lead-time materials and release the long-lead-time production items. Not having a forecast, they must guess. Unfortunately, most of those folks aren't close to the customers; they don't know about Sales' plans for promotions, pricing, sales force incentives, and the like; and thus they rely heavily on history rather than on the future outlook in the marketplace. When things go wrong, it reinforces the beliefs of the people who are saying, "You can't forecast this business. See? I told you so." **Point 1: Forecasting is being done in virtually every company. The issues are who does it and at what level it's done.**

Who Owns the Forecast?

Who's responsible for it? Who actually does the forecasting? In many companies, when I ask these questions, crisp answers rarely come back. I hear things like "it all depends which forecast you're talking about" or "well it's not very clear" or "it doesn't matter, because we use the forecast only for budgeting; we run the business on past history and hunches."

That's too bad, because one of the best ways to increase customer service levels and reduce inventories simultaneously is to do a first-rate job of forecasting. And in order to do a first-rate job, we'd better have complete clarity on whose job it is.

The issue here is accountability, and the underlying principle this: The people responsible for developing the plan (in this case the forecast, the demand plan) should be the same ones who will be held accountable for executing the plan.

Thus **Point 2: Sales and Marketing people "own" the Sales Forecast**. It's their job; they're the experts on the demand side of the business, in both planning and execution. People in other departments may support them, perhaps by operating the statistical forecasting system or otherwise generating basic data. But it's the job of the Sales and Marketing folks to review, update, and modify the Sales Forecast; they own it. They own it, because they *sell* it. They're the company's primary contact with the customers, who are — after all — the drivers of demand.

How Accurate Should the Forecast Be?

When people ask me this question, I wince. I try never to use the word *forecast* and the word *accurate* in the same sentence. Why? Because it's a turnoff for the folks in Sales who will be called upon to do the forecasting.

People who routinely criticize the forecasters for their inaccuracy might ask themselves a few basic questions. First, if the Sales people could predict the future with great accuracy, do you really think they'd be working for a living? Would they be knocking themselves out for forty or fifty or more hours per week? Of course not. If they could predict the future with great accuracy, where would they be? At the racetrack. And if the track were closed? They'd be home on their PCs, trading in stock options and speculating on pork-belly futures.

Even the best forecasts will almost always be inaccurate to one degree or another. The job of the forecasters is twofold. First, they must get the forecast in the ballpark, good enough to enable Operations people to do a proper job of initial procurement and production, capacity planning, etc.

Their second major goal is continuous improvement in reducing forecast error. In doing this, they are not trying to reach some enchanted nirvana of forecasting perfection, but to routinely produce forecasts that reflect what I call the "four R's of forecasting": forecasts that are reasoned, realistic, reviewed frequently, and represent the total demand.

Forecasting is a process. It has inputs and outputs, just like a production operation. See Figure 3-1, which shows the forecasting process in terms of inputs and outputs. Note the output — forecasts that are reasoned, reasonable, reviewed frequently, and reflect the total demand. Nowhere does it say

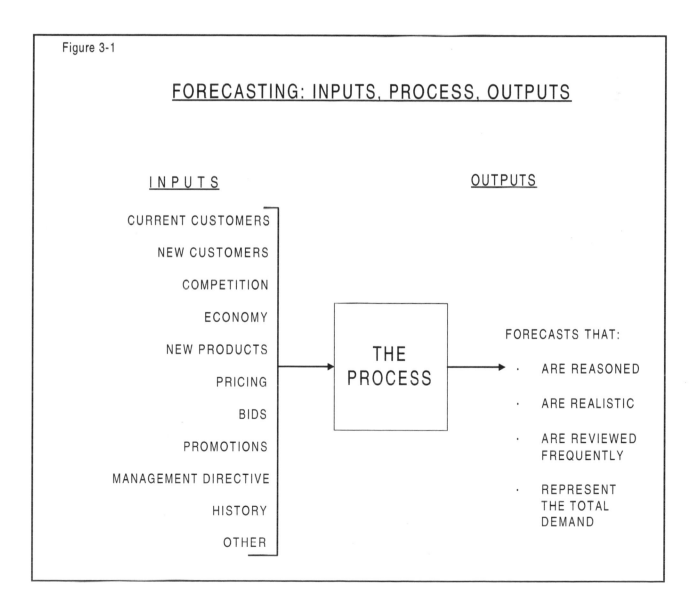

Figure 3-1

FORECASTING: INPUTS, PROCESS, OUTPUTS

INPUTS

CURRENT CUSTOMERS
NEW CUSTOMERS
COMPETITION
ECONOMY
NEW PRODUCTS
PRICING
BIDS
PROMOTIONS
MANAGEMENT DIRECTIVE
HISTORY
OTHER

THE PROCESS

OUTPUTS

FORECASTS THAT:

· ARE REASONED

· ARE REALISTIC

· ARE REVIEWED FREQUENTLY

· REPRESENT THE TOTAL DEMAND

"accurate" because talking about accuracy clouds and emotionally charges the issue. The issue is the process. **Point 3: Better processes yield better results and forecasting is no exception; better forecasting processes will yield better forecasts.**

Although I don't talk about accurate forecasts, I do promote "good" forecasts. "Good" means that the forecasters are working the process, applying their knowledge of the customers, the marketplace, future sales and marketing plans, and in general doing the best job they can.

Where Should You Forecast?

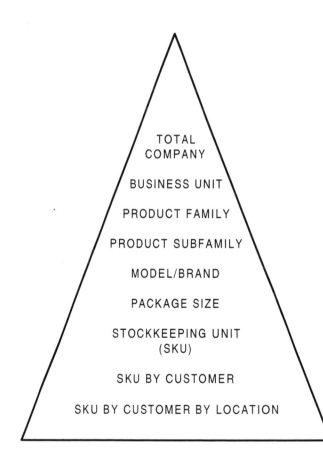

TOTAL COMPANY

BUSINESS UNIT

PRODUCT FAMILY

PRODUCT SUBFAMILY

MODEL/BRAND

PACKAGE SIZE

STOCKKEEPING UNIT (SKU)

SKU BY CUSTOMER

SKU BY CUSTOMER BY LOCATION

I don't mean where physically to forecast, as in "Should we do the forecasting in Joan's office or Doug's? Joan's got a window, but Doug's coffee is better." No, I'm talking about where in the overall product structure to forecast. In other words, at what level should you forecast? Some choices are shown on the adjacent pyramid.

Forecasting at the top of the pyramid won't work. Obviously forecasting only one set of numbers for the total company won't do the job; it's just not specific enough to provide good direction to Operations.

How about forecasting down at the bottom, stockkeeping unit (SKU) by customer by location? Well, it contains all the detail, and it gives you the capability to aggregate upwards in lots of ways. But don't jump to the conclusion that it's the best. It may be *too much* detail; forecasting at this lowest level may actually cause more forecast error, not less. One reason is that it fails to take advantage of the law of large numbers (which states that larger numbers are generally easier to forecast). Another reason is that it can be a lot more work.

One company in the spirits business learned that forecasting at the lowest possible level would be counterproductive. There was simply too much unneeded detail. For example, a case of 750 ml Old

Loudmouth Bourbon going to Pennsylvania is a different SKU from the identical product going to Ohio, because they take different case labels. While this company *stored* most of its forecasting data at a very low level, essentially SKU by customer by location, it did most of its forecasting at the brand-package size level. It has good forecasting software that allows it to easily aggregate up to brand-pack size or higher, e.g. families for Sales & Operations Planning.

So you should not necessarily forecast at the lowest level possible. Higher may be better. On the other hand, it's best to *store* the data — both actual data and forecast — at the lowest level possible, which in some companies means storing by stockkeeping unit by customer by location. That makes it possible to capture and retain very specific demand for certain customers and to view it when necessary.

For example, in the case cited above, let's say that Ohio had decided to have an aggressive promotion on 750 ml Old Loudmouth Bourbon from April through June; they anticipate that sales will be 300 percent of normal during that period. It's important to get that kind of intelligence into your formal forecasting system on a rigorous and managed basis. Being able to store forecasts at a very detailed, specific level — and then roll them up into meaningful groupings — makes that possible. That in turn can make forecasting more effective and, dare I say, more fun.

Some companies are able to forecast effectively at the family or subfamily level, and that's a good place to be. Most companies, however, do need to forecast at a somewhat lower level and then roll up the detail to subfamilies and families.

How Frequently Should You Forecast?

For a formal review, a good number is once per month. Of course, if the demand picture undergoes major changes midmonth, the forecast should be updated at the time. Forecasting less frequently than once per month can lead to the kind of problem that faced Mike, Pete, and Carol back in chapter 2.

Forecasting more frequently than once per month can work well, but before you jump into that, be sure you're doing it for the right reason. I've seen companies changing the forecast very frequently in order to effect changes directly into the near-term production line-up. Almost always this is a result of not having a good scheduling system, so they manipulate the forecast (a statement of demand) to directly affect production, which of course is supply. It is not a good practice, and it almost never yields good results.

Company S produces consumer package goods with a highly seasonal sales curve. They used to change the forecast frequently, in the very near term. What do you think the impact was on the plants? It drove them crazy. There were constant changes: stop that, start this, increase that, decrease this. As I learned more about what they were doing, I saw why: their master scheduling and plant scheduling processes were right out of the 1950s. The sales and marketing folks felt their only chance of getting the right stuff produced was to constantly change the forecast. It was the informational equivalent of using a saw to drive nails.

The good news is they don't do that anymore. They have a good resource planning system in place and can really manage their Master Schedule and plant schedules. Today they change the forecast far less frequently, run the plant more efficiently, and provide far better customer service than before.

On the other hand, some companies who excel at Continuous Replenishment (CR) update their "forecasts" a number of times per week. Typically they're receiving point-of-sale data from their larger customers, and thus can see through the customers' distribution systems right into the retail stores. They can recalculate their customers' expected demands over the next few days, reset their finishing schedules, and produce.

This is beyond the scope of most companies' capabilities today. Unless you're really good at it, go with a frequency of once per month for your forecast updates. It fits nicely with the S&OP cycle, and you can always go to a greater forecast frequency later if it will help you balance demand and supply at the mix level.

The Supply View: Capacity

The job of the people in Operations is to evaluate the new Operations Plan for "do-ability." Can we hit the numbers called for in the plan, or do they represent ten pounds in a five-pound bag? Or maybe two pounds in that five-pound bag? This is a critical step, because what's needed here is either an Operations commitment to hit the numbers in the Operations Plan or, if that's not possible, a revised Operations Plan that can be accomplished.

In some companies, evaluating a plan is easy; in others, it's more involved — and it's determined by how production resources line up with product families. We need to spend a little time here talking about how production facilities are organized.

Aligned Resources

In some cases, the production departments match up closely with the product families — Product A is made in Department A, Product B in Department B. In this situation, the capacity check can be performed right on the S&OP spreadsheet itself. Since there's a one-to-one relationship between product family and production resource, the Operations Plan for the product family represents the entire workload for the resource. The Operations people know what rates they can hit, or can gear up to hit, and it's all visible on one piece of paper. I refer to this kind of organization of manufacturing facilities as "aligned," i.e. the resources are closely aligned with the product families.

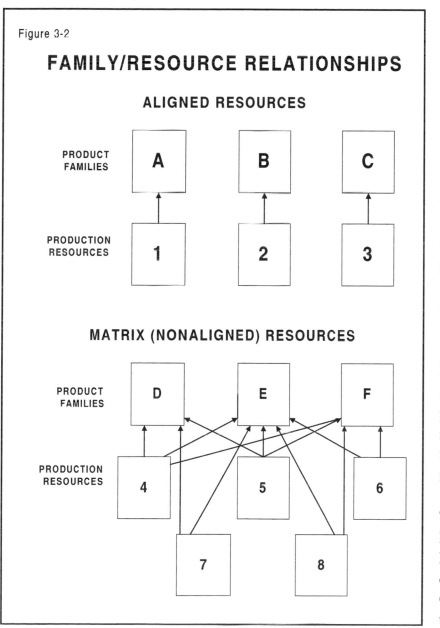

Figure 3-2

FAMILY/RESOURCE RELATIONSHIPS

Matrix (Nonaligned) Resources

In some companies, there is no tight match-up between product families and resources. A schematic of these two different approaches is shown in Figure 3-2.

The Acme Widget Company had nonaligned resources. Both of their primary product categories — Industrial and Consumer — were made in the same departments in their plant: Fabrication 1, Fabrication 2, Subassembly, and Final Assembly. A further complication was that the low end of the small and medium consumer widget families was outsourced, i.e. purchased as complete products from an outside supplier.

Try as they might, the Acme people couldn't integrate the "operations view" of the business into their product families without making the whole picture terribly complicated and user-unfriendly. They solved the problem by keeping it simple. They set up the product families and subfamilies by major category (Industrial and Consumer) and by product (small, medium, large), as shown in the left-hand column:

Families	Resources
Large Industrial Widgets	Fabrication 1
Medium Industrial Widgets	Fabrication 2
Small Industrial Widgets	Subassembly
Large Consumer Widgets	Final Assembly
Medium Consumer Widgets	Supplier A (Outsourced Products)
Small Consumer Widgets	

The resources, shown in the right-hand column, are separate elements; they represent the *supply* side of the business. Within the family groupings, Acme people first do the forecasting of future demand, and then set the Operations Plan to meet the demand and keep inventories or order backlogs at their desired levels. The Operations Plan for the individual families is then "translated" into units of workload for each resource, using a process called "Rough-cut Capacity Planning."*

---

*This is an instance in which I deviate from standard APICS terminology. The APICS Dictionary uses several terms: *Rough-cut Capacity Planning* refers to capacity planning in conjunction with the Master Schedule; *Resource Planning* and *Resource Requirements Planning* specify the process when used at the higher, Operations Plan level. Consistent with my belief that fewer terms are better, I use *Rough-cut* in both contexts, since the logic and process steps are much the same.

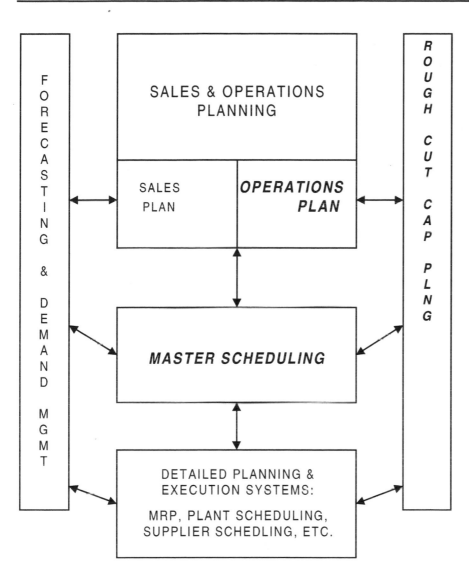

This rough-cut process enables the operations people to relate the required capacity to their available capacity. They're able to evaluate the "do-ability" of the plan, changes needed in staffing levels, the needs for new equipment, and so on.

After the newly updated Operations Plan is rearranged into aggregate departmental workloads and typically translated from units into hours, it must be displayed so that Operations people can see where their problems are. Please see chapter 12 for the details.

As with forecasting, some companies are able to do an effective job of Rough-cut Capacity Planning at the family or subfamily level. This occurs when the families or subfamilies are fairly homogenous, i.e. when the individual items within them create a similar load on the resources. Other companies find they need to build up the Rough-cut Capacity Plan from a detail level, typically the Master Schedule, because the individual products place widely differing loads on the resources.

Demand/Supply Strategies

It's necessary to define an operating approach for each product family, and we refer to such approaches as *demand/supply strategies*. These strategies spell out whether the product family is make-to-stock or make-to-order, what the target customer service levels are, and what the desired level of finished goods inventory or customer order backlog is. These inventory and backlog targets are essential: along with the forecast, they drive the Operations Plan.

In Figure 3-3, we can see two examples of demand/supply strategies. In this example, Acme Widget has said that the Medium Consumer Widget family contains primarily make-to-stock products, that it wants to provide 99 percent on-time and complete customer service for these products, and that doing so will require ten days of finished inventory.

Figure 3-3

EXAMPLES OF DEMAND/SUPPLY STRATEGIES

Product Family: Medium Consumer Widgets

1. Make-to-Stock
2. Target Customer Service Level: 99% Line Item Fill
3. Target Finished Goods Inventory: 10 Days Supply

Product Family: Large Industrial Widgets

1. Make-to-Order
2. Target Customer Service Level: 98% Order Fill
3. Target Customer Lead Time: 4 Weeks

Large Industrial Widgets are make-to-order products. As such there is no finished goods inventory for them; rather the variable here is the size of the customer order backlog, which directly determines the customer lead time.

Let's look at that target customer service level for Medium Widgets. It says 99 percent Line Item Fill. That means that 99 percent of all line items are to be shipped on time and complete. That sounds fine until you consider that Acme Widget averages five line items per customer order, and most orders call for items from different families. The measure that should be used to track customer service, I submit, should not be line fill but rather order fill — the percentage of customer orders shipped on time and complete.

So what is Acme doing messing around with line item fill in this demand/supply strategy business? The answer is: they have to. You see, the strategies are specific to a family, and they drive the forward planning logic of S&OP. But the important customer service measure is order fill. Acme recognized that. Early in their Executive S&OP meeting, they addressed overall customer service performance using order fill statistics. Their order fill target is 95 percent. In order to reach that, since they average five items per order, they set their line fill target at 99 percent.

Setting the targets for inventory and order backlog is, for most companies, an imprecise science. Unless you have very good data readily available, you can't get highly accurate here; don't make a career out of trying to decide what they should be. Regarding the size of the finished goods inventory, my advice is to get started in S&OP by setting the targets at roughly what you have now — unless they're obviously much too high or low. Then, as you move through time and improve your processes, you can adjust them — usually downward.

Part of the issue here involves mix — how many different line items are in a given family. Let's take two product families, A and B. Everything about these two families is the same except for one thing: Family A has 4 items and Family B has 400. Which family would require the larger safety stock to give the same level of customer service? If you said A, guess again.

For make-to-order products, the target customer lead time is largely a function of the customer order backlog, which in turn is typically a trade-off between the desire to get the product to the customers quickly and the amount of time needed for pre-production, production, and post-production activities. Here also, my general recommendation is to get started with roughly what you're doing now, and then sharpen it up as you go along.

Sometimes a tough question to answer is whether a company is make-to-order or make-to-stock. For purposes of Sales & Operations Planning, many companies who initially think they're make-to-order are actually make-to-stock. Let's take Company D as an example. They make shopping bags, among other things, for retailers. Many of their bags are customer-specific; they show the customer's name: Nordstrom, Abercrombie and Fitch, Brooks Brothers, and so on. Sounds like make-to-order, right? Well, not quite. Company D has "stocking agreements" with many of its customers that require certain levels of finished goods inventory. For S&OP this is a make-to-stock product, not a make-to-order one. The question is not primarily whether the product is built for one customer only, but rather whether the product typically goes to a finished goods inventory after it's produced. If the latter, it's a make-to-stock product for our purposes here.

Commercial aircraft manufacturers are largely make-to-order. They finish producing the plane for a given airline, take it up for a test hop, slap a green sticker on it, and away it goes. That's make-to-order. Company D's shopping bags, for S&OP purposes, are make-to-stock.

Time Fences

Many companies using S&OP have a ground rule that says, "The current month is a done deal." They mean that there's not much possibility of changing production rates *economically* within the current month. Now keep in mind, they're talking about volume. Mix is different; it's easier to change schedules close in as opposed to overall run rates.

Will companies using S&OP ever change volumes close in? Yes, if the needs of the business require it and if the costs of not changing exceed the costs involved in making the change. But normally they'll try to avoid making close-in rate changes.

This is a simple example of a time fence. A slightly more complex example might be:

- Hold the current month.

- Month 2 (in the future) — changes +/– 20 percent are okay.

- Month 3 and 4 — changes +/– 30 percent are okay.

- Month 5 and 6 — changes +/– 40 percent are okay.

- Month 7 and beyond — open.

For companies needing a more formal time fence structure like these, it's a good ideal to spell them out in the Sales & Operations Planning policy.

Please note: people can decide to override time fences. Time fences are there mainly to serve as guides for decision-making and to help avoid jerking the plant around unduly. One of the plant's jobs, I submit, is to become increasingly flexible so that it can respond *economically* to close-in changes. That makes for happy customers and happy colleagues in Sales and in Finance.

To sum up, setting demand/supply strategies means spelling out what you're trying to accomplish with each product family in terms of demand and supply. Here are some questions that play into this:

- Is this family make-to-stock or make-to-order?

- What is the target customer service level for this family? This refers to on-time and complete shipments to customers.

- If the family is make-to-stock, what is the target finished goods inventory level? In other words, how much inventory is needed to enable the target customer service level?

- If the family is make-to-order, what is the target customer order backlog? Remember, in the make-to-order world, backlog — negative inventory — is a key factor; it determines how long it will take for customers to get their product from you.

This is important. These demand/supply strategies — simple statements of goals and targets — spell out what we need to do to keep our customers happy and to effectively manage our finished inventories and order backlogs. They direct us in balancing demand and supply. They're necessary for S&OP because they play a key role in the logic of the spreadsheet. In addition, as we'll see in chapter 14, they help to keep the need for continuous improvement visible as the company goes through time.

FREQUENTLY ASKED QUESTIONS

We have several pieces of equipment that are really bottlenecks. They're individual machines, not entire production departments. Can we do Rough-cut Capacity Planning on them?

Absolutely. These individual units are resources, perhaps small in size but big in impact. For S&OP purposes (overall volume), treat them as production departments. Some companies, in order to deal with these kinds of issues, will do Rough-cut Capacity Planning off the *Master Schedule,* rather than off the higher-level Operations Plan, so that they get a more focused picture.

You can go further. If you need to schedule these kinds of resources very tightly, you should probably consider some of the excellent finite scheduling software that's available today.

Chapter 4

The Monthly S&OP Process

The essence of Sales & Operations Planning is decision-making. For each product family, a decision is made on the basis of recent history, recommendations from middle management, and the executive team's knowledge of business conditions. The decision can be:

- change the Sales Plan,

- change the Operations Plan,

- change the inventory/backlog plan, or

- none of the above: the current plans are okay.

The decisions form the agreed-upon, authorized plans by the president, all involved vice presidents, and other members of the Executive S&OP Team. They are documented and disseminated throughout the organization. They form the overall game plan for Sales, Operations, Finance, and Product Development. (New product plans are reviewed within S&OP in terms of their impact on the demand and supply picture.) These groups break down the aggregate plans from S&OP into the necessary level of detail: individual products, customers, regions, plants, and materials.

Sales & Operations Planning, however, is not a single event that occurs in a two-hour Executive S&OP meeting each month. Rather, preliminary work begins shortly after month's end and continues for some days. The steps involve middle management and some others throughout the company (see Figure 4-1). They include:

- updating the Sales Forecast;

- reviewing the impact of changes on the Operations Plan, and determining whether adequate capacity and material will be available to support them;

- identifying alternatives where problems exist;

- identifying variances to the Business Plan (budget) and potential solutions;

- formulating agreed-upon recommendations for top management regarding overall changes to the plans, and identifying areas of disagreement where consensus is not possible; and

- communicating this information to top management with sufficient time for them to review it prior to the Executive S&OP meeting.

Thanks to the work that's gone before, the Executive S&OP meeting should not take a long time — two hours or less is the norm with companies that do this well. The net result of S&OP for the top management group should be less time in meetings, more productivity in their decision-making processes, and a higher quality of work life. And most of the middle-management people involved in the earlier Pre-SOP processes will experience the same benefits. Let's take a look at each of the steps shown in Figure 4-1.

Step 1 — Run Sales Forecast Reports

Most of this activity occurs within the Information Systems department, and it happens shortly after the end of the month. It consists of three elements:

- Updating the files with data from the month just ended — actual sales, production, inventories, and so on.

- Generating information for Sales and Marketing people to use in developing the new forecast. This could include sales analysis data, statistical forecast reports, and worksheets for field sales people.

- Disseminating this information to the appropriate people.

To make S&OP a timely process overall, it's important that this step be completed within just a day or two after the end of the month.

Step 2 — The Demand Planning Phase

This is where people in Sales review the information they received from Step 1, analyze and discuss it, and generate the new management forecast for the next twelve or more months. Please keep in mind: this forecast must include both existing products *and* new products. Let's look at two very different businesses and see how the forecasting process might be carried out.

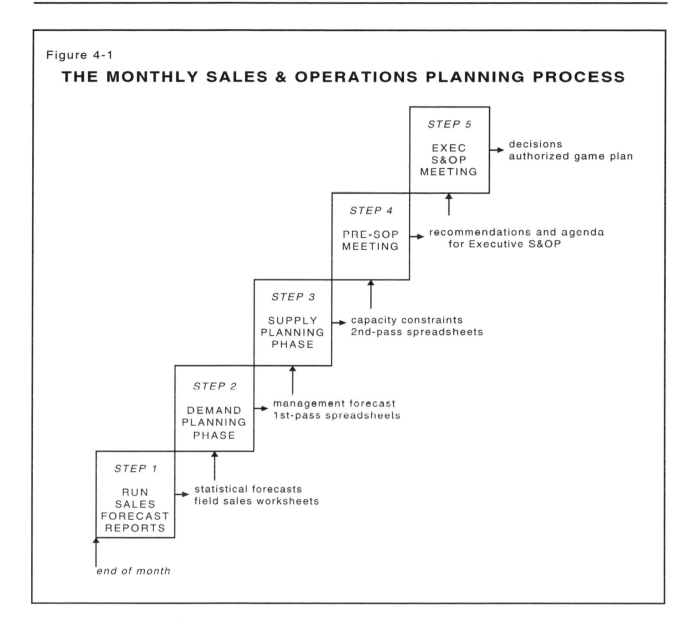

Figure 4-1

THE MONTHLY SALES & OPERATIONS PLANNING PROCESS

STEP 5

EXEC S&OP MEETING → decisions authorized game plan

STEP 4

PRE-SOP MEETING → recommendations and agenda for Executive S&OP

STEP 3

SUPPLY PLANNING PHASE → capacity constraints 2nd-pass spreadsheets

STEP 2

DEMAND PLANNING PHASE → management forecast 1st-pass spreadsheets

STEP 1

RUN SALES FORECAST REPORTS → statistical forecasts field sales worksheets

end of month

The Acme Widget Company has two divisions: Industrial and Consumer. The Industrial business is largely a make-to-order operation, with relatively few customers taking almost all of the volume. In this business, a very large portion of the forecasting task is customer contact: learning from the key customers their future plans for the use of Acme's products. Statistics on past sales can be helpful but the key is to capture what the customers think is going to happen. The biggest help that good information can provide to the field Sales people is to show, by customer, what products they've taken in the past and to give the Sales folks an easy way to input new forecasts into the system.

The Consumer Division, on the other hand, is almost totally a make-to-stock business. There are many customers and, except for several mass merchandisers, no one customer makes up a large percentage of the Consumer Division's sales volume. The foundation for forecasting these products is statistical forecasting; Acme Widget has an effective statistical forecasting package that uses past history as a basis for statistical projections of future forecasts.

I hasten to add that the forecasting process for the mass merchandisers and other large customers should look more like a make-to-order process than make-to-stock; the field Sales people must be in direct and frequent contact with their customer contacts regarding future needs.

Let's look at how the Demand Planning phase takes place within the Consumer Division. After the statistical forecast reports are generated, the information is reviewed by managers in the Sales and Marketing areas. Their job is to override the statistical forecasts where appropriate. When would it be appropriate? Any time that past history is not the best predictor of the future. What factors would make history not the best predictor? Well, quite a few:

- field input regarding large customers
- new products
- promotion plans
- price changes
- competitive activity
- industry dynamics
- economic conditions.

It's the job of people in Sales and Marketing management to use their knowledge of these factors and possibly others to come up with the *management* forecast. That is their responsibility. And, actually, it's also in their best interest. Most often, the management forecast proves to have a lower error rate. (Okay, it's more "accurate.") Why? I believe it's because the statistical forecast is based heavily on past history.* As long as the future is going to be exactly like the past, then everything works. But usually it's not. Changes in the above factors can all make the future different from the past. It's the job of the *people,* using their God-given intelligence and their knowledge of current conditions, to override the statistics and get the best forecast possible.

---

*Some powerful statistical forecasting routines exist that take into account factors such as economic indicators, consumer attitudes, and industry trends. If you're using one of these tools, great; you're a leg up. However, my point here still applies: human judgment by knowledgeable people is essential.

Acme Widget would follow a slightly different process for its Industrial Division and for the large customers in the Consumer Division. The key to forecasting this business rests less on statistical projections and more, as we said, on capturing the customers' plans for Acme products. What's needed is the involvement of the field sales force in capturing those plans and an efficient process to communicate the information from the field into the general office.

For any kind of business, involving the folks in New Product Development is important here. They typically have the best handle on timing of new product launches; Sales should have already made forecasts, and their forecasts should be reviewed for possible changes. The resulting statements of new product demand must be included here so that the Supply people can make the appropriate plans.

The forecasts of future demand are best made in units and then translated into dollars, although it can be done the other way around if necessary (see chapter 8). Regardless, it's critical that there be a dollar view of the updated forecast before it goes further. Frequently, people from Finance and Accounting participate in this update, and in my experience their participation is very valuable in this Demand Planning step.

Since the output from Demand Planning is the management-authorized forecast, it's necessary to get the senior Sales and Marketing executive into the loop. In some companies, the forecasters make a brief presentation of the updated forecast to the Vice President of Sales and Marketing. Bringing the senior executive into the process at this point does several things:

- It allows him or her to ask questions, challenge the numbers, and if need be change some of them.

- It avoids surprises at the S&OP meeting.

- It results in a truly "management-authorized forecast," one that all of the key players have bought into. They've signed off on it. This forecast, then, represents Sales' best estimate of future demand.

So how does the new forecast enter into the S&OP spreadsheets? One good way to do it is, first, to roll forecast, production, and inventory data inside the spreadsheet one month to the left, to reflect the passage of time. Then lay in the newly updated forecasts along with actual sales, production, and inventory data for the month just ended. The result is what I call the First-Pass Spreadsheets.

You now have the new forecast playing against the old Operations Plan, and the resultant inventory or backlog numbers will now be different. Some families will probably change very little, but others will show major differences from last month, because of last month's demand, changes to the forecast, inventory adjustments, and shifts in the backlog. This set of First-Pass Spreadsheets now goes into the Supply Planning step.

Do companies have a formal Demand Planning meeting? Some do and some don't. In general, larger companies tend to hold a formal meeting to get the management forecast nailed down, while frequently smaller companies have a series of smaller, somewhat less formal face-to-face sessions. In either case, the final review by the senior Sales and Marketing executive is essential.

Step 3 — The Supply (Capacity) Planning Phase

The newly updated S&OP spreadsheets are the primary input to the Supply Planning phase, which is Operations' responsibility.

Their first step is to modify the Operations Plans for any families or subfamilies that require it. If little or nothing has changed from last month, then there's probably little reason to change anything this month. On the other hand, changes in the Sales Forecast, inventory levels, or the size of the customer order backlog can readily trigger a change to the Operations Plan.

Outputs from the Supply Planning step are the Second-Pass Spreadsheets, Rough-cut Capacity reports, and a list of any supply problems that cannot be resolved or that require decisions further up the ladder. In some cases, demand (as expressed by the forecast) simply exceeds supply by too great a margin to reach; the constraints cannot be overcome within the time allowable. Sometimes these constraints are within the company's production resources; at other times constraints may exist elsewhere in the supply chain, i.e. the outside suppliers.

At other times, acquiring the resources necessary to meet the demand may be feasible but will require spending that can be authorized only by top management. These are the kinds of issues that the supply folks carry into the Pre-SOP meeting.

As with Demand Planning, some companies will conduct a formal meeting for this Supply Planning step, while others find it more effective to simply work the process informally one on one.

Step 4 — The Pre-SOP Meeting

Objectives of the Pre-SOP meeting include:

- making decisions regarding the balancing of demand and supply;

- resolving problems and differences so that, where possible, a single set of recommendations can be made to the Executive S&OP meeting;

- identifying those areas where agreement cannot be reached, and determining how the situation will be presented in the Executive S&OP meeting;

- developing, where appropriate, scenarios showing alternate courses of action to solve a given problem;

- setting the agenda for the Executive S&OP meeting.

The key players in this meeting typically include several of the people from the Demand Planning phase, including someone from Product Development, Operations people from the Supply Planning step, one or more representatives from Finance, and the S&OP Process Owner (see chapter 7).

Their job is to do a family-by-family review of the Second-Pass Spreadsheets, including subfamilies where they exist, and to make adjustments where appropriate. They also check for resource constraints, using either the product family/subfamily spreadsheets or separate capacity displays. Where there are constraints, demand priorities must be established and that, of course, can only be done by Sales and Marketing people.

In addition, their review should look at actual performance to plan for sales, production, inventories and backlogs, and once per quarter a check on the demand/supply strategies for each family to make appropriate changes (see chapter 14).

The outputs from the Pre-SOP meeting include:

- An updated financial view of the business, including matching the latest sales call to the business plan for the total company. (This is typically done on a rolled-up, dollarized spreadsheet covering all families.)

- A recommendation for each product family, contained on a Third-Pass Spreadsheets, as to the future course of action:
  — stay the course, no change;
  — increase/decrease the Sales Plan; and/or
  — increase/decrease the Operations Plan.

- New product launch issues not covered within the product family review.

- A recommendation for each resource requiring a major change: e.g. add people, add a shift, add equipment, offload work to a sister plant, outsource, or reduce the number of people or shifts.

- Areas where a consensus decision could not be reached, possibly as a result of disagreement or where competing alternatives might be "too close to call." In such cases, it's often very helpful for alternative scenarios to be presented — Plan A, Plan B, Plan C — with dollar data as well as units, to show the financial impact.

- Recommendations for changes to demand/supply strategies, where appropriate.

- Agenda for the S&OP meeting.

On the next page, there's an example of an agenda that has worked well for some companies.

To sum up, the Pre-SOP meeting is a "get-ready" session for the Executive S&OP meeting. But it's actually a lot more than that, because the Pre-SOP is a *decision-making* session. The mindset that the Pre-SOP participants should have is, "If this were our business, what would we decide to do?"

Step 5 — The Executive S&OP Meeting

This is the culminating event in the monthly S&OP cycle. Its objectives are:

- To make decisions on each product family: accept the recommendation from the Pre-SOP Team or choose a different course of action.

- To authorize changes in production or procurement rates, where significant costs or other consequences are involved.

```
SAMPLE AGENDA

EXECUTIVE
SALES & OPERATIONS PLANNING
MEETING


1.    Macro Business Review

2.    Customer Service Performance

3.    New Products

4.    Family-by-Family Review and Decisions

5.    Production/Procurement Rate Changes

6.    Collective Impact on Business Plan

7.    Recap of Decisions Made

8.    Critique of Meeting
```

- To relate the dollarized version of the S&OP information to the Business Plan and where they deviate, decide to adjust the Sales & Operations Plan and/or the Bus- iness Plan, as appropriate.

- To "break the ties" for areas where the Pre-SOP Team was unable to reach consensus.

- To review customer service performance, new product issues, special projects, and other issues — and make the necessary decisions.

Outputs from the Executive S&OP meeting include the meeting minutes, which spell out the decisions that were made; modifications to the Business Plan, if any; and the Fourth-Pass Spreadsheets, which reflect changes made at the Executive meeting.

All these things taken collectively form the company's authorized game plan. As such, there is urgency to get the word out to all involved people, and for this reason I recommend that the meeting minutes and the Fourth-Pass Spreadsheets be distributed within two working days of the meeting.

Here's a quick point for those of you in smaller companies. You may not need to have both a Pre-SOP meeting and an Executive S&OP meeting. In some companies or business units, perhaps around $25 million or less per year, the line between operating managers and executives gets blurred. The operating-level managers report directly to the general manager. I've seen some companies in this category combine the Pre-SOP and Executive S&OP meetings into one — and it's worked well. What is called for, in that case, is a general manager with a fair amount of patience, because there's no Pre-SOP session to get all the ducks in a row.

FREQUENTLY ASKED QUESTIONS

What if there's a major event — affecting demand and supply — that occurs shortly after the Executive S&OP meeting? It doesn't make sense to wait another whole month to address such a big issue.

It certainly doesn't. Many successful S&OP users, when confronted with such situations, will go through an abbreviated, accelerated S&OP process. They'll go through the Pre-SOP steps very quickly, focusing only on those parts of the business that are affected. Then, within a day or two, they'll conduct the Executive S&OP session and make the necessary decisions.

Throughout the abbreviated process, they try to keep the steps, the report formats, and the decision-making process the same — because the people are familiar with those processes and know they're solid.

Part Two

How to Make It Work

Chapter 5

The S&OP Implementation Path Overview

Would you agree that what you've seen so far is fairly simple? No brain surgery, no orbital dynamics, no advanced calculus. But there's a paradox here: even though this process itself is very straight-forward and easy to understand, it is *difficult* to implement it successfully. Here's why:

- It's a new process for the company.

- New processes mean change.

- Change, in this context, means people changing some aspects of how they do their jobs.

- People need a solid understanding of the process and a vision of the future in order to willingly and enthusiastically make the necessary changes.

- Top management people are typically very busy and thus have a low tolerance for spending time on unproductive activities. Progress must be made quickly and consistently. If that doesn't happen, the implementation project may stall out and never reach a successful conclusion.

So it's hard to do this right. The good news is that, when you implement it, you don't need to reinvent the wheel. There is a proven implementation path, developed over the years by trial and error. It's easy to follow (even though there's a fair amount of work involved). If you do it correctly, you can have near-100 percent assurance that your implementation of S&OP will be successful.

Please take a moment and look at Figure 5-1 on the next page. It contains the generalized S&OP Implementation Path, which shows a number of tasks to be completed, some sequentially and some in parallel. It indicates that the time required for a complete implementation will be about nine months for the average organization. Here also, there's a bit of a paradox. Why does something that involves relatively few people take six or eight or ten months to implement? It's because of the nature of the S&OP process. It occurs on a monthly cycle. During implementation, incremental experience and expertise are gained only once each month.

For almost all of the companies I've observed over the years implementing S&OP, benefits come sooner than six months. The reason lies in S&OP's ability to provide that window into the future mentioned in chapter 1. Take another look at Figure 5-1.

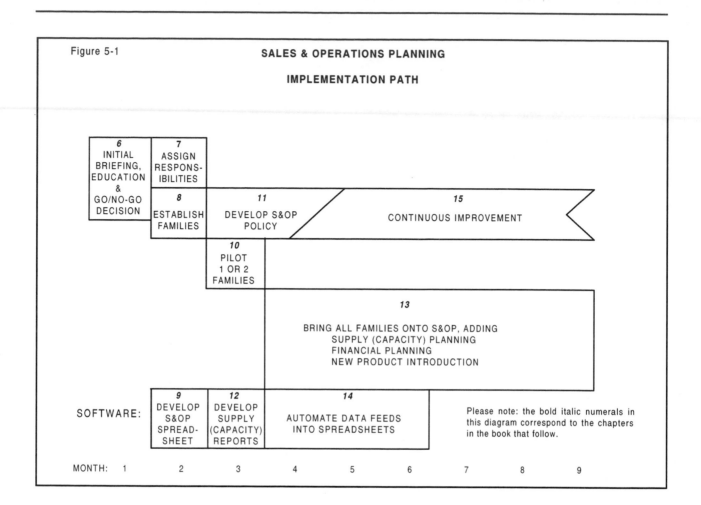

Figure 5-1

SALES & OPERATIONS PLANNING

IMPLEMENTATION PATH

Check the third row down — Pilot 1 or 2 Families — and the fourth row — Bring All Families Onto S&OP. Almost invariably, in about month two or three, people are able to see things that they wouldn't have without S&OP. It's common to hear comments like, "Golly. If we weren't doing this, we'd have had a big problem four months from now on Medium Widgets." Being able to get a better focus on the future means that problems can be avoided by taking early corrective action.

There's more to the S&OP Implementation Path than a diagram. In appendix A, you'll find a verbal version of the Implementation Path diagram. It is a generalized outline for companies to use to tailor their own project schedule for implementation. Doing so, I believe, will get you through the project sooner, more completely, and more successfully.

Therefore, as soon as possible after steps 6 and 7, develop your detailed project schedule and get concurrence from all of the key players.

Two things to keep in mind regarding S&OP implementation:

- Even though the logic of S&OP is simple, implementing it is not. Implementing it requires people to make changes — to do some aspects of their jobs differently — up to and including the senior executive in charge of the business.

- Because of the monthly cycle, it will take about eight months to implement basic Sales & Operations Planning.[*] Benefits, however, will start to be realized much sooner.

In the chapters that follow, we'll discuss each of the boxes in the Implementation Path diagram shown in Figure 5-1. Please note that the individual boxes in the diagram are coded to the chapters that follow.

---

[*] "Basic Sales & Operations Planning" refers to the process as we've defined it in part one, chapters 1 through 4. Advanced elements include, among other things, global S&OP and the integration of S&OP with powerful Advanced Planning Systems (APS) to enhance simulation and scenario development. See chapter 17.

Chapter 6

Initial Briefing, Education, & Go/No-Go Decision

Virtually all business processes center around people, and S&OP is certainly no exception. We've been saying for years that people are the A item, as in ABC — Pareto's Law. The B item is data, and the computer is the C. Very simply, people are by far the most important element in Sales & Operations Planning, and thus the people part of the project must be done very well.

Initial Briefing — Making the Business Case

For most companies, the best way to get started with S&OP is to conduct an initial briefing — at the executive level. This is a one- to two-hour session facilitated by an S&OP-knowledgeable person. Its purpose is to transfer enough information about the process to enable the senior management group to readily:

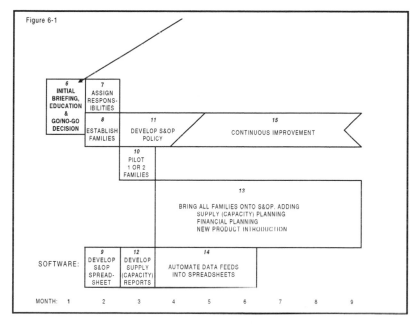

Figure 6-1

- Understand the capabilities of Sales & Operations Planning. They need to learn what it does, how it works (in very general terms), and what kinds of benefits companies have realized from using it.

- Match S&OP's capabilities to their business problems. This is where the business case is made for Sales & Operations Planning. What problems is the company experiencing in shipping to its customers on time, running the plants effectively, and keeping finished goods inventories low and customer order backlogs in line? Which of these would get better if S&OP were used well?

- Develop a rough-cut benefit statement, in dollars. What would be S&OP's impact on the bottom line?

- Make an informed decision to proceed, or not proceed, to the next step — the education day.

Please note: nowhere here does it say to make a decision on whether or not to implement S&OP. That choice follows the education day. Rather, the decision here is merely to go to the next step. These sessions work best with relatively few people — the top management team plus a few others — and when they're held around a conference table.

One last point. In some companies, it's possible to skip the initial briefing and go right to education day. This could be the case where some key people have already learned a bit about S&OP at a seminar, or where the president has prior S&OP experience and is convinced of its merits, or where there's been enough informal talking and reading about S&OP that the senior management group is comfortable with the concept. But while it's okay to skip the initial briefing, it's *not* okay to skip the education day.

Education Day

There are two main reasons for taking a day to learn about Sales & Operations Planning. First, people need to learn a good deal about this process before they can make an informed decision about implementing it. Second, an education session establishes a common framework, viewpoint, and terminology for the people who will be involved in operating Sales & Operations Planning.

This session should involve all of the people who will be "hands on" with S&OP — top management, middle management, and others, e.g. forecast analysts, sales people, planners, and schedulers. Since S&OP is easy to understand, this event does not need to take a long time — a half-day or full-day session conducted in-company should be adequate.

But, there's a pitfall here. Don't be blind-sided by the simplicity of the logic of S&OP. Don't make the mistake of thinking that because it's not complicated people don't need to learn about it. The reason gets to the fundamental objectives of the education day.

One objective is fact transfer — to learn the logic of S&OP and how it's supposed to work. That's easy. Far more difficult, and far more important, is the other objective of this education step: behavior change. It goes like this:

- Sales & Operations Planning is a new process for the company.

- Implementing new processes means change.

- Change means people, including top management, changing the way they do their jobs.

The primary objective of this education session, therefore, is for the people to gain that solid understanding of the S&OP process and to see the compelling business reasons for it — in order to willingly and enthusiastically make the necessary changes, including some aspects of how they do their jobs.

This is as true with top management as with any other group in the company. The reason is decision-making. Making the right decisions today is tougher than ever because of the rapid pace of change. As we said earlier, better processes yield better results. Better decision-making processes yield better decisions. And that's what much of the top management job is all about: making better decisions — making decisions more productively, on a more timely basis, and with higher quality — than the competition's executives. Executives and everyone else to be involved need to understand that S&OP is a superior decision-making process; it helps people make better decisions. Therefore it's a very important tool for both top and middle management. And thus those folks need to learn about it.

So, you might be thinking, whom do we get to present this session? Well, there's bad news and good news here. The bad news is that the number of *knowledgeable, qualified* people — with hands-on, successful S&OP implementation experience — is small. When you're talking to someone regarding your S&OP education session, or other S&OP support, I recommend strongly that you check his or her references. You need positive answers to the following kinds of questions:

- Have you been involved in one or more implementations of Sales & Operations Planning?

- How successful were those implementations?

- What were your roles in those implementations?

- Where were those implementations, and can I talk to the companies?

- Do you have a process, a methodology for implementing S&OP?

Go/No-Go Decision

Following the education session, I recommend that the Executive S&OP Team plus other involved people get together and make a formal go/no-go decision on S&OP. If the decision is no, for whatever reason, then the case is closed. Let's go do something else.

Most of the time, the answer is yes, let's do it. I believe the main reason is that the inherent logic of S&OP is valid and compelling; for most top management people, it exerts a strong pull. I can remember the CEO of a consumer packaged goods company, upon learning about S&OP at the education day, saying, "If we'd had this 25 years ago, I'd be a younger man. I'd have fewer scars — and more hair."

FREQUENTLY ASKED QUESTIONS

In our company, we're doing much of S&OP, but without top management. We've tried to get them to have an initial briefing with no luck. They won't read the books or even the articles. What should we do?

What you should *not* do is give up. Keep your S&OP process going. Where practical, start to display your S&OP spreadsheets in meetings with top management. Try to present recommendations within the framework of the S&OP display. Use the same format to present alternative scenarios to support difficult decisions.

Further, try to enlist an executive champion and work with him or her to move the process upward in the company. Your executive champion might be successful in getting a standing time slot, say twenty or thirty minutes, once a month at an executive staff meeting. Use this to recap the Pre-SOP meeting. After this has been happening for a few months, start asking the executive group to ratify the decisions made in the Pre-SOP.

I think that steps like these and perhaps others might pay off in the long run. And the downside risk seems to be almost nonexistent.

Chapter 7

Assign Responsibilities

Once the decision is made to proceed, it's time to get the project organized. Here's what needs to be addressed in terms of roles and responsibilities.

Executive Champion/Sponsor

It's important to have one executive assigned to champion the S&OP project. He or she can be a big help in keeping top management attention focused on the project, removing impediments, acquiring needed resources, and in general supporting the S&OP Process Owner and the other folks doing the heavy lifting.

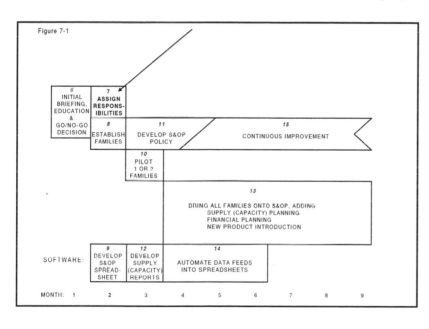

Who should it be? In general, my first choice would be the president — provided he or she has the time and the inclination. If not the president, then take your pick from any one of the VPs. Ideally the person selected would be enthusiastic about Sales & Operations Planning and would have a solid working relationship with the president.

S&OP Process Owner

There needs to be a process owner, someone who will lead the implementation project and, most often, continue in a process leadership/ownership role over time. This is normally not a full-time job. You won't need to free someone up from all other duties to do this.

So what should this person look like and from where in the organization should he or she come? I don't believe it should be a top management person (primarily for reasons of time availability) but it should be someone with solid managerial experience. The person should have good people skills, be pro-active and well organized, and be able to lead a meeting effectively. He or she should know the business — the people, the products, the processes, and last but not least the customers. Do not fill this role with an outside hire; it will take an outsider a long time to learn these critically important elements of your business.

Okay, so where should the S&OP Process Owner come from: Manufacturing, Sales, Marketing, Purchasing, Finance? My answer is: Take your pick. S&OP Process Owners I have known include:

- Director of Sales Administration

- Demand Manager

- Materials Manager

- Production Control Manager

- Controller

- Sales Manager and Production Control Manager (a joint, shared assignment).

At Company A, Ken had been on board for about eight years and was the Production Control Manager at their largest plant (one of four). Ken is a self-starter, and before S&OP came onto the company's radar screen he had already started doing some S&OP-like planning for his plant. When the company decided to go with a formal Sales & Operations Planning process, he was tapped to head up the project and the process. He moved from the plant to the corporate office, became responsible not only for S&OP but also for forecasting, and now reports to the Director of Sales.

Company R's general office was in Connecticut with its manufacturing headquarters located in Kentucky. There were dual S&OP Process Owners, one for each location. At the general office, the Director of Sales Administration led the effort, while the Process Owner at the manufacturing headquarters was the Director of Materials Management. They were in frequent contact and shared meeting facilitation responsibilities at both the Pre-SOP and Executive S&OP meetings.

One of the first jobs for the S&OP Process Owner and Executive Champion should be to address the implementation project schedule as discussed in chapter 5. A process that works well is to:

1.   Prepare a tentative, rough draft of the schedule.

2.   Circulate the draft to all involved people.

3.   Get their feedback and make the appropriate changes.

4.   Publish the schedule.

5.   Track progress against the schedule.

6.   Report on the project's status at each Pre-SOP and Executive S&OP meeting.

Spreadsheet Developer

You might find this curious — to include what might seem to be a rather mundane function. Perhaps, but I learned the hard way not to overlook it. In chapter 9, we'll get into the spreadsheet topic in depth, but for now let's just say that the odds are very high that your S&OP information will be displayed on spreadsheets generated by Excel, Lotus 1-2-3, or Quattro Pro. Setting them up will be somewhat complex. But that's not all. During the first six months of implementing S&OP, you will probably change them at least four or five times. The changes won't usually be major, but they will require some time and effort. I've found it helpful to have one person designated as the developer and maintainer of the spreadsheet.

An interesting possibility: if your S&OP Process Owner is reasonably good with spreadsheets then perhaps he or she could handle this task.

Demand Planning Team

People with the following kinds of job titles typically populate the Demand Planning Team:

Demand Manager	Customer Service Manager
Product Manager	Sales Administration Manager
Forecast Analyst	Accounting Manager
Sales Manager	New Products Coordinator
Sales Person	S&OP Process Owner

Please note: these are generic job titles. They probably won't match up exactly with yours. Moreover, they are only examples; not all of them should be considered as mandatory. In a typical company, there are normally about a half dozen to a dozen people involved in the demand planning/forecasting process.

As we saw in chapter 3, the senior sales and marketing executive should serve as a resource to the Demand Planning Team, approving or modifying their forecasts each month before they're passed to the Supply Planning Team.

Supply Planning Team

This group is made up of people such as:

Plant Manager	Production Control Manager
Materials Manager	Accounting Manager
Purchasing Manager	New Products Coordinator
Master Scheduler	S&OP Process Owner
Distribution Manager	

Most of the comments made for the Demand Planning Team apply here also. Not all of these jobs need to be represented in the process. Formal meetings are held in some companies, not in others. The senior operations executive might serve as a resource to authorize the output from this group.

Pre-SOP Team

The Pre-SOP team includes folks such as:

Demand Manager	Plant Manager
Materials Manager	Purchasing Manager
Customer Service Manager	Accounting Manager
Forecast Analyst	Controller
Product Manager	New Products Coordinator
Master Scheduler	S&OP Process Owner

Don't be put off by the apparent size of this group. Yes, there are a dozen job titles identified here, but frequently several functions are performed by the same person.

On the other side of the coin, in some jobs there will be more than one person, e.g. three product managers and two plant managers. Therefore, it's possible that you would wind up with a group that's a bit larger than what you're used to. At that point, you either drop people off the team, or get started with the larger group and see what happens.

I'm more comfortable with the second option. To me it's far better to have a group slightly larger than ideal than to exclude people who can contribute to the process. One factor in favor of the larger size is that these meetings are not brainstorming sessions. Rather, they're structured meetings with a high degree of focus on the process. Virtually all of the players will have already participated in one or both of the prior steps, so there won't be a large number of surprises or new issues to work.

Executive S&OP Team

This group should include at a minimum the:

President (General Manager, COO)
Vice Presidents of:
      Sales
      Marketing
      Operations
      Product Development
      Finance
      Logistics
      Human Resources
S&OP Process Owner

Most Executive S&OP Teams I've been involved with are not this small. Rather, they include other people who can add value to the process, such as the Demand Manager, Product Manager, Sales Manager, Customer Service Manager, Plant Manager, Materials Manager, Master Scheduler, Supply Planner, Controller, and New Product Coordinator. The comments that I made for the size of the Pre-SOP team apply here also.

A company not far from where I live was implementing S&OP. The two plant managers were on their Pre-SOP team but were not included in the Executive S&OP meeting, in order to keep the group small. At the time, the company was facing a number of tricky capacity issues, and they found that their Executive S&OP meetings were difficult and not as productive as they could have been. They just didn't have enough plant-specific knowledge in the room to make decisions crisply. They added the two plant managers, and things went a lot better.

Consulting Support

Here's some more good news: unlike some other initiatives, with S&OP you won't need to have an army of outsiders — systems integrators, junior consultants, or whatever — swarming all over your company. On the other hand, support from an S&OP-knowledgeable person can be a big help in making this process work. This consultant's role is to teach, to encourage, to head off problems before they occur, to help solve problems that have occurred, to keep the project on the rails, to push — hard, if necessary — for visible progress each and every month so that the project doesn't stall out.

Not an enormous amount of the consultant's time should be required to do that. For a typical company, an average of two days per month for about eight months has proven to be adequate — with more than two days per month being applied early in the process and fewer later.

Among companies that have used this kind of outside expertise, the percentage of successful implementations is very high. Among companies that haven't done so, the success rate is much lower. The comments I made in chapter 6 about qualified people to conduct your initial education session also apply here.

FREQUENTLY ASKED QUESTIONS

What about setting up an S&OP project team or task force? Can this be helpful?

It may be. In larger companies, where the operating environment tends to be more complex, this can be helpful. For a business of average size and complexity, I've not found it to be necessary. What needs to be managed and accomplished can typically be handled well by the Executive Sponsor and the S&OP Process Owner working with the Demand, Supply, Pre-SOP, and Executive S&OP teams themselves.

****

Does everyone have to sit through the entire meeting (Pre-SOP or Exec), or can people come and go as needed?

For me this question is more relevant for the Pre-SOP meeting, which can be lengthy. I've seen it work well for the folks from, say, Plant A to be in the first part of the meeting, followed by the Plant B people. But please note: if Plants A and B make some of the same products and have similar resources, this approach might not work. When workload needs to be reassigned, you really need both groups in the room at the same time.

Product managers might need to stay only as long as their products are being discussed — provided also that there's no significant interrelationship or capacity conflicts between their products and those of some other product manager. The same goes for New Product Development. The Finance representative would probably be there for the entire session, as would the Demand Manager, Materials Manager, S&OP Process Owner, and others.

I don't think this question is germane for the Executive S&OP meeting. That session lasts no more than two hours, and it's the meeting that gives overall direction to the business. Two hours or less seems to me to be a very good investment of people's time.

Chapter 8

Establish Families, Subfamilies, and Resources

Here are some of the issues to keep in mind when setting up your product families and resources.

Families — How Many?

If you have more than about a dozen product families, you probably have too many. Why? Well, it gets down to the mission of S&OP: it's a decision-making process for top management to use in balancing demand and supply.

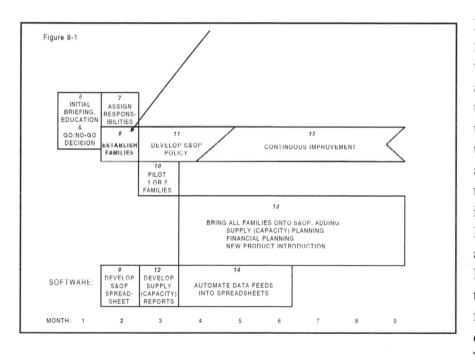

Having worked with numerous top management teams over the years, I can assure you of several of their characteristics: first, they're very busy; second, they therefore have limited attention spans; and third, they are therefore not interested in getting into lots of detail unless it's absolutely necessary. Having to review twenty or thirty or more product families once each month does not fit that profile. Thus, if you have too many families, top management will tune out. If top management tunes out, the process will die. Hands-on, active participation by top management is essential for this decision-making process to be effective.

The best number of product families is around six to twelve. When you start to get much above that, you're probably asking for trouble.

Families — How to Select Them

Many companies, prior to getting into S&OP, have their product families effectively identified. In their budgeting and business planning processes, the families are spelled out, and they make perfectly good sense. If you're in that category, great. Use what you have for S&OP.

In other companies, they haven't yet spelled out a good product family array and doing that is an important early step. Among the options here are to structure your product families by:

- product type (scotch, bourbon, gin)

- product characteristics (high performance, standard)

- product size (large, medium, small)

- brand (Taurus, Contour, Focus)

- market segment (industrial, consumer)

- customer.

The fundamental question is, simply, how do you go to the marketplace? Acme Widget's products, for example, fall logically into Industrial and Consumer, and then into subdivisions — small, medium, and large — within those two.

Companies with make-to-order products will sometimes set up their families by customer, with perhaps the 20 percent of customers who account for 80 percent of the business spelled out as individual families and the remaining low-volume customers grouped into one family.

Making Use of Subfamilies

How, you may be thinking, is it possible to define a complex business in just a few families? My question for you is: What is your purpose? If you're talking about filling customer orders and making shipments, you need to work with individual products and customer orders. However, you can't do Sales & Operations Planning at that level even if you wanted, because S&OP is a tool for *aggregate* planning. Its focus is on *volume,* not mix.

TOTAL COMPANY

BUSINESS UNIT

PRODUCT FAMILY

PRODUCT SUBFAMILY

MODEL/BRAND

PACKAGE SIZE

STOCKKEEPING UNIT (SKU)

SKU BY CUSTOMER

SKU BY CUSTOMER BY LOCATION

In chapter 3, we discussed at which level to forecast, and we identified the possibilities shown at the left. Obviously we can't do S&OP at the very top of the pyramid, because there's not enough granularity at that level upon which to base demand/supply decisions. Towards the bottom of the pyramid, there's too much detail; we're flying fifty feet off the ground at 400 knots. We're surely not going to see the big picture down there.

There's an area in this pyramid that sits below the high-level product families used in the Executive S&OP meeting and above individual products, and we refer to these intermediate groupings as "subfamilies." For example, the Acme Widget Company, as we saw, has two product lines — Industrial and Consumer. Within each category, there are three product families: small, medium, and large. The Consumer product line has a further subdivision: seasonal and everyday. Acme people often need to view these separately; the seasonal line requires extensive early production prior to the onset of the peak Christmas selling season, while demand and production for everyday products is of course more stable. When planning the pre-build, with its attendant rise in inventory, top management people want to see the plan so they can approve it. They also want to view it during the height of the season. However, during most of the year, it's not of interest to them *unless something is going wrong.*

It's the job of the Pre-SOP Team to monitor the subfamilies to ensure that they're performing to plan. When they're not, the Pre-SOP people need to fix them, and sometimes that requires a decision (e.g. for reasons of cost, impact on other parts of the business, or staffing levels) from top management. In such cases, the Pre-SOP Team is empowered to elevate a subfamily, along with their recommendation, to the Executive S&OP meeting for a decision. This has the dual advantages of keeping the top management folks in the loop when needed, but not taking up their time unnecessarily.

Product Families And Nonaligned Resources

Products are what the company provides to its customers, and a company's families should be organized on that principle. Set up your families based on what makes sense to the folks in Sales and Marketing. Make sure the families line up with market segments, customer groups, or, when appropriate, individual large customers. When you do that, you'll probably find that your families *do not line up with your resources* — plants, departments, and processes. That's because most companies don't have aligned resources.

That's okay. Don't make the mistake of trying to force-fit the resource picture into your product families. The result is usually a mish-mash that doesn't do a good job. Rather, identify your non-aligned resources separately and view their status by means of the Rough-cut Capacity Planning process we talked about in chapter 3.

Unit of Measure

When setting up your product families, it's necessary to specify the unit of measure to be used for each family. Choices for unit of measure include:

- each

- cases

- thousands

- thousands of cases

- gallons

- liters

- pounds

- kilos

- tons.

For most companies, selecting the units of measure is a no-brainer. On the other hand, some companies really struggle over this issue. Here also, the point about separating demand and supply applies: pick the units of measure based on how you go to the marketplace. Then, if operations needs something different, derive that with Rough-cut Capacity Planning.

FREQUENTLY ASKED QUESTIONS

How about using dollars as the primary unit of measure?

Only as a last resort. Certainly we need to see dollars because the financial view is essential for running a business well. But it's far easier to go from *units to dollars* than the reverse. So the message is: plan in units and translate to dollars.

There are, however, times when it's just not possible to use units. One electronics company I'm familiar with had product families with processors, monitors, modems, readers, power supplies, and on and on. There was simply no common unit of measure that spanned all the diverse products within a given family. Therefore, they used dollars because they had no choice. And it worked well.

****

Does it ever make sense to have the product families based on how Operations views things?

Only if that arrangement also works for Sales. If so, what you probably have are aligned resources. If that arrangement doesn't seem to work well for Sales, then the key questions include:

- Will it be more difficult for Sales to do a good job of forecasting?

- Will it be more difficult for Sales to relate the S&OP process to how they go to market and how they work with customers?

If the answer to either of these is yes, it will be more difficult for Sales, then I recommend not doing it.

Chapter 9

Develop S&OP Spreadsheet

We had a preliminary look at several S&OP spreadsheets in chapter 2. Now it's time to get into the details and understand how they work. We'll get started with the sample spreadsheet in Figure 9-2.

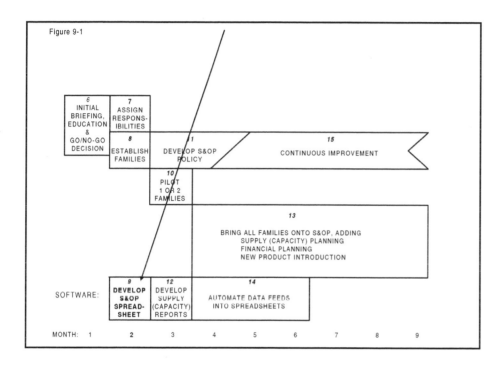

Figure 9-1

6 INITIAL BRIEFING, EDUCATION & GO/NO-GO DECISION	7 ASSIGN RESPONS-IBILITIES	
	8 ESTABLISH FAMILIES	1 DEVELOP S&OP POLICY

15 CONTINUOUS IMPROVEMENT

10 PILOT 1 OR 2 FAMILIES

13 BRING ALL FAMILIES ONTO S&OP, ADDING
SUPPLY (CAPACITY) PLANNING
FINANCIAL PLANNING
NEW PRODUCT INTRODUCTION

SOFTWARE:

9 DEVELOP S&OP SPREAD-SHEET

12 DEVELOP SUPPLY (CAPACITY) REPORTS

14 AUTOMATE DATA FEEDS INTO SPREADSHEETS

MONTH: 1   2   3   4   5   6   7   8   9

Make-to-Stock Format

In this example, for a make-to-stock product family called Medium Widgets, the demand/supply strategy specifies a target customer service level (shipments on time and complete) of 99 percent. The target finished inventory necessary to support this shipping performance has been set at 10 days' supply. See the area in Figure 9-2 identified by *A*. Let's examine the 10-day inventory target. Why does this company feel it needs 10 (work) days of finished goods inventory? The answer is that its experience over the recent past has shown that 10 days is a minimum level necessary to provide 99 percent customer service.

Should this 10-day supply target be considered a constant, fixed far out into the future? Not at all. The principle of continuous improvement should drive this company to improve its sales, production, and logistics processes so that 99 percent customer service is attainable with only, say, 9 days of supply. And then 8 days. And then 7. But for now, the realities of life are that it takes about a half month's worth of inventory to provide the 99 percent service level.

In *B,* actual sales are compared to forecast. For the past three months, sales are running ahead of forecast by 44,000 units. Actual production performance to the plan is evaluated in *C*. It's close to being perfect.

Figure 9-2	THE ACME WIDGET COMPANY -- SALES & OPERATIONS PLAN FOR OCT 1999

FAMILY: MEDIUM WIDGETS (MAKE-TO-STOCK)   UNIT OF MEASURE: 000 UNITS

TARGET LINE FILL: 99%   **A**   TARGET FIN INV: 10 DAYS

B HISTORY   **E**

SALES	J	A	S	O	N	D	J	F	M	3rd 3 MOS	4th 3 MOS	NEXT 12 MONTHS	5th + 6th 3 MOS	FISCAL YEAR LATEST CALL	BUSINESS PLAN
OLD FORECAST	200	200	200	200	200	200	200	200	200	660	660	2520	1320	CALL	PLAN
NEW FORECAST				210	210	220	220	220	220		690	2670	1470	$25,540	$25,400
NEW VS. OLD FCST				10	10	20	20	20	20	30	30	150	150		
ACTUAL SALES	222	195	227												
DIFF: MONTH	22	-5	27												
CUM		17	44												

OPERATIONS **C**   **F**

OLD PLAN	200	200	200	210	210	200	200	200	220	660	660	2540	1320
NEW PLAN				210	220	230	230	230	230	690	690		
NEW VS. OLD PLAN					10	30	30	30	10	30	30		
ACTUAL	200	206	199										
DIFF: MONTH	0	6	-1										
CUM		6	5										

INVENTORY **D**   **G**

PLAN	100	100	100	60	70	80	90	100	110	110	110
ACTUAL	78	88	60								
DAYS SUPPLY	8	9	6	6	6	7	8	9	10	10	9
LINE FILL %	97%	98%	89%								

DEMAND ISSUES AND ASSUMPTIONS   **H**

1. FORECAST RELECTS LAUNCH OF NEW
      DESIGNER WIDGET LINE IN 3RD QTR.
2. ASIA FORECASTED TO REACH 1996 VOLUME

SUPPLY ISSUES   **J**

1. XMAS FULL PLANT SHUTDOWN RESCHEDULED 1
      STAGGERED PARTIALS THRU FALL AND WINTER

Area **D** shows inventory performance to plan, and the actual customer service performance. We can see a serious problem developing here: as the forecast was oversold, the actual inventory dropped below plan. The result is that customer service has dropped to 89 percent for September, quite far below its 99 percent target.

The new Sales Forecast is shown in **E**. Towards the right of the page are shown a total for the next twelve months, and totals in units and dollars for the fiscal year, ending in December in this example.

As a result, the fiscal totals are made up of both sales history (Jan–Sept) and Sales Forecast (Oct–Dec). Farther to the right is the forecasted dollar amount in the Business Plan. This latter number allows for an easy comparison between the Business Plan and the S&OP forecast for the fiscal year's volume. On the basis of this, the top management team will probably elect to change the Business Plan accordingly.

Also in *E,* please note that the old forecast is shown in addition to the new forecast. Many companies like to do this so they can see the magnitude of the changes. The same approach is being taken in the Production section, comparing the old plan with the new.

The assumptions that underlie the forecast are listed in area *H,* in the lower right-hand corner. The future Operations Plan, based on the new forecast and other considerations, is shown in *F,* and the relevant supply (production/procurement) issues are listed in *J.*

Area *G* contains the future inventory projection for finished goods, both in units and days-on-hand. The unit calculation is:

Last month's ending inventory (e.g. end of September: 60)

minus

This month's new Sales Forecast (October: 210)

plus

This month's new Operations Plan (October: 210)

equals

This month's ending inventory (October: 60)

The projected days-on-hand calculation is:

Next month's new forecast (e.g. November: 210)

divided by

Number of work days in month
(We're using a straight 20 per month in this spreadsheet.
In chapter 12, we'll see a spreadsheet with varying work days per month)

equals

Daily sales rate (210/20 = 10.5)

divided into

This month's inventory plan (October: 60)

equals

This month's days' supply (October: 5.7, rounded to 6)[**]

In summary, Figure 9-2 is an example of a proven, effective format for Sales & Operations Planning. The intent is to have all of the relevant information for a given product family on one piece of paper. That enables each family's situation to be viewed completely and organically, both its recent past and its future outlook. For decision-making purposes, this has proven to be far superior to individual displays of information that focus only on sales, or on inventory levels, or on production.

A caution: as you get started, try not to get the spreadsheet too "busy." It's easy to keep adding this piece of data and that piece, until the display gets very crowded and hard to read. Keep it simple, at least in the beginning. There'll be plenty of time to add things later.

Make-to-Order Format

A spreadsheet for a purely make-to-order family isn't treated much differently from make-to-stock (see Figure 9-3). As we saw in chapter 2, the main difference is that the spreadsheet for make-to-order doesn't contain data for finished goods inventory. That's because there is none. (If there were, then the family wouldn't be purely make-to-order.) Rather, the inventory numbers are replaced by a display of the customer order backlog — both past and projected.

The other difference is that, in projecting the backlog into the future, the calculations are reversed from make-to-stock. In make-to-order, demand is added to the projected backlog and production is subtracted from it. (In make-to-stock, demand is subtracted from the projected inventory, and production is added to it.)

[**] In prior months, actual inventory is used rather than plan. In our example, July's actual was 78, August 88, September 60, yielding the days supply numbers of 8, 9, and 6 respectively.

Figure 9-3   THE ACME WIDGET COMPANY -- SALES & OPERATIONS PLAN FOR OCT 1999
FAMILY: LARGE WIDGETS (MAKE-TO-ORDER)   UNIT OF MEASURE: EACH
TARGET LINE FILL: 99%   TARGET ORDER BACKLOG: 4 WEEKS

	HISTORY										3rd	4th	NEXT 12	LATEST	BUSINESS
BOOKINGS	J	A	S	O	N	D	J	F	M	3 MOS	3 MOS	MONTHS	CALL	PLAN
OLD FORECAST	20	20	20	20	20	20	20	20	20	60	60	240	$1,800M	$1,800M
NEW FORECAST				20	20	20	22	24	24	72	72	274	$2,055M	$1,800M
NEW VS. OLD FCST				0	0	0	2	4	4	12	12	38	$255M	
ACTUAL BOOKINGS	22	20	21	20	20	20	8							
DIFF: MONTH	2	0	1											
CUM		2	3											
PRODUCTION/SHIPMENTS														
OLD PLAN	20	20	20	20	20	20	20	20	20	60	60			
NEW PLAN				20	21	22	24	24	24	72	77			
NEW VS. OLD PLAN				0	1	2	4	4	4	12	17			
ACTUAL	20	21	20											
DIFF: MONTH	0	1	0											
CUM		1	1											
ORDER BACKLOG														
OLD PLAN		30	30	30	30	30	30	30	30	30	30			
NEW PLAN					30	29	27	25	25	25	25	20		
ACTUAL	28	30	29	30										
BACKLOG -- # WEEKS				6	6	5	5	5	5	5	4			
ORDER FILL %	99%	100%	100%			10% TIME FENCE								

DEMAND ISSUES AND ASSUMPTIONS   SUPPLY ISSUES

1. FORECAST RELECTS INCREASED   1 UNABLE TO REACH 4 WEEKS BACKLOG UNTIL AUGUST BECAUSE OF:
   SALES BECAUSE OF PROBLEMS AT   A) FORECAST INCREASE, AND
   COMPETITOR PLUS SHORTER   B) NEW EQUIPMENT NEEDED TO GO BEYOND 24 UNITS PER
   LEAD TIMES.   MONTH NOT AVAILABLE UNTIL JULY

Here's how the projected backlog calculation works:

Last month's ending backlog (e.g. end of September: 30)

plus

This month's new bookings forecast (October: 20)

minus

This month's new operations plan (October: 20)

equals

This month's ending backlog (October: 30)

I used a simplified calculation for the number of weeks of backlog, as follows:

New forecast (e.g. November: 20)

divided by 4 (weeks in a month) equals

Weekly forecast (5)

divided into

Ending backlog (October: 30)

equals

Backlog in weeks (October: 6)

Here again, with both make-to-order and make-to-stock, my advice is to keep the spreadsheet as uncluttered as possible.

One last point regarding the make-to-order spreadsheet: in this example, we're showing a time fence at the end of the third month into the future. It's labeled "10% time fence," which means that production rate changes within the first ninety days should be held to 10 percent or less. As with all time fences, it should be considered as a guideline only and not a hard and fast rule. Typically it will mean that overriding the time fence carries significant costs or other penalties, so a decision to change it should be made thoughtfully and by the right people.

FREQUENTLY ASKED QUESTIONS

Why does the spreadsheet need to project so far out into the future? What benefit is a forecast for twelve or fifteen months or eighteen months out?

One reason is Financial Planning, and there are two pieces to it:

- We need at least twelve months forward visibility, called the "planning horizon," to compare the S&OP plan with the Business Plan for the current fiscal year. Early in the fiscal year, we'll need forecasts that "reach" to the year's end in order to do that.

- Further, we're going to begin work on next year's budget about three to six months prior to the start of the next fiscal year. At that point, we'll need the three to six months of forecast for the current year, plus twelve months for next year. Having this forward forecasting and planning information in the ongoing business planning process makes the entire budgeting cycle much less time-consuming and, dare I say, less painful. One CEO I worked with said that one objective in implementing S&OP was to free people from having to spend large amounts of time in budgeting, so they could focus on the important stuff: serving the customers, developing new products, and running the plants more flexibly and effectively. That works for me.

Another reason for a long planning horizon, of course, is for Operations people to get some feel for what their capacity needs will be down the road. If each month they're looking at a potential bottleneck out in the future, they will be able to start to think about it, kick around some ideas, and check out some possibilities in advance of having to make decisions. A pilot friend of mine said once that S&OP helps to "get your head out of the cockpit" so you can look out longer range.

****

Isn't it confusing to display so much information on one page?

It can be, if the display is not well designed. It's a balancing act between showing the necessary elements and not showing information that's not essential. I suggest you start off with a mindset that "less is more." Include only the information you feel is necessary; then you can add the "nice-to's" as you go along.

Is it really necessary to use the spreadsheets in the Executive S&OP meeting?

I believe it is. The spreadsheets are the heart of the entire process: it's on that document that all of the major demand and supply issues come together and can be viewed holistically.

****

Okay, then is it necessary to view all the spreadsheets in that meeting, or could we just look at the families where something has changed and a decision is needed?

For the first year or so, I recommend that you look at all of them. Then, after you're really proficient at the process and you'd like to speed things up, you might give it a try. But keep an open mind — you may decide it's better to cover them all.

Chapter 10

Pilot One or Two Families

Thus far in our S&OP implementation journey we've learned about Sales & Operations Planning, assigned responsibilities, set up the product families, and developed a first draft of the spreadsheet. Now it's time to get started on the actual process itself, and before we launch right into it, we need to ask ourselves a few questions.

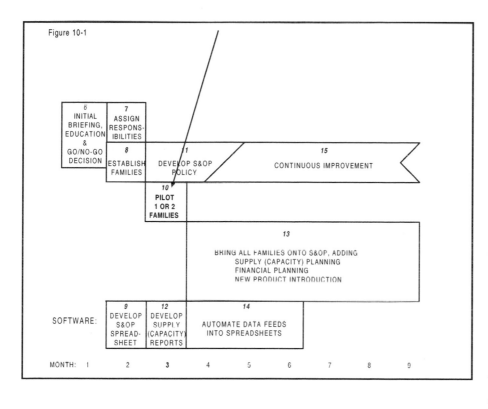

Figure 10-1

First, what's the best way to do this? Broadly, we have two choices: start up using all families, or pilot one or two families. The title of this chapter tells you which one I prefer. The reason I prefer the pilot approach is that trying to do more than one or two families will very likely be overwhelming. It's enormously easier to focus on only one or two families.

Which family should you pick, the hardest one or the easiest?* Here I opt for the middle of the road. Don't pick the most complicated or trickiest product family, because you might have a really tough time getting it off the ground. If your production resources are matrix rather than aligned, I suggest you avoid a family with capacity problems. Keep in mind that the main mission in this early stage is not to get operational results but rather to implement a process and get it working. On the other hand, I'd be reluctant to pick a simple family that represents, say, less than 2 percent of the total business. It just doesn't have enough impact to get people excited.

---

*The decision we're addressing here — which family or families to pilot — should actually be made earlier, when the project schedule is first developed. By that time, following the Education step (covered in chapter 6), people should know enough to make a solid decision on the pilot.

I suggest you look at the three or four product families that are most important to the company. The importance could be based on sales dollars, margin contribution, impact on customers — or possibly on which families are giving you, and perhaps your customers, the most problems. Within those three or four families, pick one that's not highly complex and get started.

Finally, is one product family enough? After all, the title of this section references "one or two" product families. Why would you want more than one to get started? Well, think back to the Acme Widget Company. They have two business units: Industrial and Consumer.

The two units have very different products; they sell into very different markets; they have separate marketing and sales staffs; and their forecasting processes are quite different. Piloting only one family, say Medium Consumer Widgets, would mean that the folks in Industrial would not have much involvement with S&OP for the entire month. In this case, I'd suggest to Acme that they pick two families: one from Consumer and one from Industrial.

Once you've selected the pilots, and accomplished the tasks in the earlier steps, it's time to just do it. What's needed here is to simply follow those steps in the monthly S&OP process, which is diagramed on the next page.

1. **Run sales forecast reports.** First, run the reports and worksheets that you use to update the Sales Forecasts, and get them to Sales so they can get started on the Demand Planning phase.

   In addition, get the numbers for actual sales, production, and either inventory or customer order backlog. You'll need them for the last three months if you use the spreadsheet format recommended in this book. Ideally you can also pick up a fiscal year-to-date number for actual sales and production.

   Enter the data into the spreadsheet. Down the road this data-entry function must be automated because of the volume. However, for now, most companies will enter the data manually if there will be any delay at all waiting for the feeds to be automated.

   At the same time, the demand/supply strategy data — target customer service levels, target finished goods inventories for make-to-stock products, and target customer order backlogs for make-to-order — must be entered.

2. **Demand Planning Process.** While this is going on, the Demand Planning phase can kick in. Sales generates forecasts for the pilot family. The forecasts are entered into the S&OP spreadsheet, which then goes to Operations.

3. **Supply Planning Process.** Here Operations lays in the Operations Plan for the pilot family. This is set to meet the Sales Forecast and to get the inventories or backlogs to their target level. Also, Operations needs to verify that the Operations Plan is "do-able" or, if not, how much of it can be achieved and what are the options to provide the rest of the needed product.

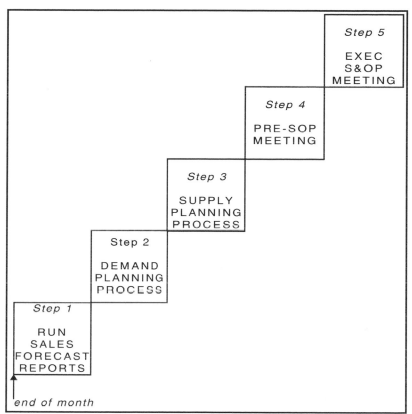

4. **Pre-SOP Meeting.** This is where the two groups formulate their recommendations to the Executive Team, discuss any data problems that need to be fixed, and set the agenda for the Executive S&OP meeting.

5. **Executive S&OP Meeting.** Here decisions regarding the pilot family are made, feedback is solicited from the group for improvement, minutes are distributed, and so on.

That's it. You've just completed your first S&OP cycle and, if you did your homework and followed the path outlined in this book, the odds are good that it was reasonably effective. It started your company down the learning curve, and you positioned yourselves for a better, easier cycle next month — when you'll be adding more families.

A caveat: don't try to get the material for the first Executive S&OP meeting to a point of perfection. Rather, in preliminary conversations with the Executive Team, the level of expectations should be set along these lines:

- This is the first step in the implementation process. It won't be perfect and may not even be highly polished. Be patient. It will get better in a hurry. I guarantee it.

- We don't have all the data we need — but we have enough to get started.

- We're working to get all the data, but it'll take a bit longer and we didn't want to delay the implementation waiting for it.

Who's the best person to carry this message to the Executive Team? The Executive Champion, who of course is a member of that group. These are some of the most important things he or she can do:

- Set the level of expectations,

- Keep S&OP on the front burner with high visibility, and

- Run interference for the Pre-SOP people and others regarding such things as resource allocation.

My experience with top management groups is that they tend to be quite understanding of start-up problems and will be supportive. What they will be unhappy about is seeing the same problems month after month. Making consistent progress over time is far more important than the level of polish of the first Executive S&OP meeting. It should be good, but doesn't have to be great.

Tips for Effective Executive S&OP Meetings

Over time your meetings should become very effective. Here are some ideas to help you achieve that.

- **Send out the agenda in advance.** Getting the agenda out several days before the meeting gives the participants a chance to see what decisions they'll be asked to make.

- **Include the important S&OP spreadsheets with the agenda.** This will give the participants a chance to review status on the major product families and resources.

- **Use a projector at the meeting.** This focuses the group's attention, keeps everyone on the same page, and helps people to better understand the pros and cons of the decisions they're making.

- **Have enough "Pre-SOP People" at the Executive S&OP meeting to answer likely questions.** Having to scramble to get information or to reconvene the meeting later represents inefficient use of the Executive Team's time.

- **Have a pre-appointed minute-taker.** This person should be someone other than the facilitators or presenters.

- **At the end of each meeting, take five minutes to review the decisions made.** This ensures that all of the decision-makers heard the same thing and understand the decisions coming out of the meeting.

- **At the end of each meeting, take five minutes to critique the process.** Each participant should be asked for comments. This step speaks to continuous improvement and helps to ensure that the meetings get better and better.

- **Distribute the minutes within two work days of the meeting.** This meeting sets the company game plan for the upcoming months, so there should be a sense of urgency to get the word out as to what those plans are.

Chapter 11

Develop S&OP Policy

Lots of people feel the same way about rules and regulations as I do. I'm not wild about 'em. Having said that, I hasten to add that a formal Sales & Operations Planning Policy is necessary for the successful implementation and operation of the process. It doesn't have to be anything fancy, and with luck it will fit on one piece of paper. (Twist my arm and I'll agree to two pages, but absolutely no more.) This document should spell out:

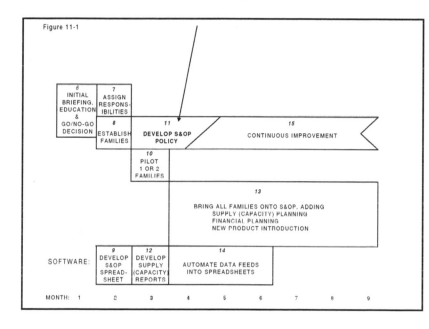

Figure 11-1

- the objectives of the company's Sales & Operations Planning process

- the steps in the process

- the participants in each step of the process

- actions to be taken at each step.

I recommend that this document be signed by the president and others as appropriate.

On the next page is an example of an S&OP policy patterned after one developed by a company I'm familiar with. Please note: This company held formal meetings in its Demand Planning and Supply Planning phases. They were dispersed geographically and thus had to have prearranged meeting times so that all participants could be there, either in person or by conference call. As we said earlier, other companies don't find it necessary to have formal meetings in these early steps; rather, they work the process in individual face-to-face or telephone sessions.

ACME WIDGET COMPANY — SALES & OPERATIONS PLANNING POLICY

Sales & Operations Planning establishes the overall level of sales and manufacturing output, expressed in families, to form the company game plan. Its primary purpose is to establish rates of activity that will achieve the company's objectives, including: meeting customer service and revenue goals, raising or lowering inventories and customer order backlogs, maintaining a stable work force, and enhancing the effectiveness of new product introductions.

1. The Executive S&OP meeting will be held monthly in conjunction with the scheduled Officers' meeting. Attendees:

President/CEO	Vice President Operations
Vice President Finance/CFO	Vice President Product Development
Vice President Marketing	Vice President Sales
At least two members of the Pre-SOP Team	

Actions include: resolution of open issues from Pre-SOP, authorization or modification of Pre-SOP plans, changes to the Business Plan, New Product issues, and others as appropriate.

2. The Pre-SOP meeting will be held monthly on the third Friday following the prior fiscal month's close. Attendees:

Controller	Logistics Manager	Product Development Managers
Customer Service Manager	Master Schedulers	Product Managers
Demand Manager	Plant Managers	Sales Administration Manager
Forecast Analyst		

Actions include: development of plans to ensure a balance of demand and supply, formulation of recommendations for Executive S&OP, development of agenda for Executive S&OP, review of long-term capacity constraints, and obsolescence issues. Considerations will include: customer service levels, market strategies, inventory goals, current forecasts and backlogs, new product strategies, financial plans, current status, and capacities.

3. The Supply Planning meeting will be held monthly on the third Wednesday following the close of the previous fiscal month. Attendees:

Capacity Planner	Demand Manager	Plant Managers
Controller	Master Scheduler	Purchasing Manager

Actions include: review of Capacity Planning information resulting from the new forecast, review of material availability and lead time problems, manpower planning issues, cost absorption issues arising from production rate changes, and problems with new product introductions and obsolescence.

Any critical resource — manpower, equipment, supplier — whose required capacity varies from its demonstrated capacity by more than +/– 5% must be reviewed for action and possible discussion at the Pre-SOP meeting.

4. The Demand Planning Meeting will be held monthly on the second Friday following the close of the previous fiscal month. Attendees:

Controller	Distribution Planners	Product Managers
Customer Service Manager	Logistics Manager	Sales Administration Manager
Demand Manager		

Actions include: approval of a forward 24-month unit and dollar forecast, review of product family trends, new product introduction issues, and special product and customer demands.

Authorized: _____ _____ _____ _____President
        Vice President   Vice President   Vice President   Vice President

Revision #: _____   Effective Date: _____

Chapter 12

Develop Supply (Capacity) Reports

This section applies mainly to companies whose production resources are organized on a matrix basis. If you have aligned resources, you won't need separate capacity reports. How so? Well, since all of the output from a given resource (department, plant, supplier) goes to only one product family, then the spreadsheet for that family can display all that department needs to know about the future workload for that resource.

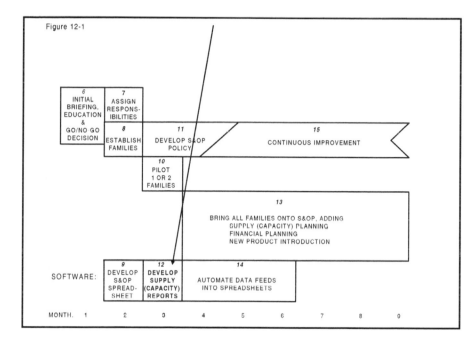

Figure 12-1

Look at the spreadsheet for Company A shown in Figure 12-2 for an example. You can see that, in the section labeled "Operations," there are rows for :

- production days per month

- daily production rate (required to hit the plan)

- Operations Plan (Line 1 times Line 2).

Their focus in the Supply Planning phase is to verify that they can hit the daily rates their plan is calling for. When they say "yes," that means they're making a commitment to hit that plan. That commitment will be noted in the Executive S&OP meeting.

I happened to attend the Executive S&OP meeting where this spreadsheet was addressed. The president pressed the Vice President of Operations and the Plant Manager: "Are you guys sure you can get 43,000 per day?" The answer came back: "Yes sir. You can count on it." But there's more to it than just making a commitment. Operations's commitment and all others are reviewed at the following month's meeting, when actual results are compared against plan. This is serious stuff.

Figure 12-2	COMPANY A -- SALES & OPERATIONS PLAN FOR MARCH	
FAMILY:	XRS	UNIT OF MEASURE: 1000 UNITS
TARGET LINE FILL:	99%	TARGET FIN INV: 10 DAYS ON HAND

	HISTORY									3rd 3 MOS	4th 3MOS	NEXT 12 MONTHS	LATEST CALL	BUSINESS PLAN
SALES	D	J	F	M	A	M	J	J	A					
NEW FORECAST	750	725	724	978	802	784	939	825	811	2584	2446	10169	$27,240,918	$21,411,776
ACTUAL SALES	714	794	762											
DIFF: MONTH	-36	69	38											
CUM		33	71											
OPERATIONS														
PRODN DAYS/MO	*21*	*20*	*20*	*25*	*19*	*19*	*24*	*20*	*20*	*62*	*62*			
DAILY PRODN RATE	*32.3*	*39.7*	*41.1*	*43.0*	*41.0*	*40.5*	*40.5*	*40.5*	*41.0*	*40.7*	*40.5*			
OPERATIONS PLAN	*614*	*794*	*800*	*1075*	*779*	*770*	*972*	*810*	*820*	*2530*	*2511*	*10267*		
ACTUAL	679	794	822											
DIFF: MONTH	65	0	22											
CUM		65	87											
INVENTORY														
PLAN		307	337	284	433	410	396	429	414	423	369	434		
ACTUAL	302	267	267	327										
DAYS-ON-HAND		7	7	9	10	10	10	10	10	10	9	11		
LINE FILL %		72%	88%	91%										

Companies with matrix resources don't have it quite so easy. They will need to use the Rough-cut Capacity Planning tool that we saw in chapter 3. But this also isn't open heart surgery. It is not orbital dynamics. It's merely a straightforward grouping of production workload into resources and a comparison of the supply of capacity with the demand for it.

To see how this works, let's look at the display on the next page. It shows a Rough-cut Capacity report from Company F, a foundry, whose products are all make-to-order and are sold primarily to machinery manufacturers. The resource in question is a primary manufacturing department that makes products from a wide variety of different product families.

In this example, the squares represent the *supply* of capacity: the department's demonstrated capacity at 240 hours per month, below which they don't want to drop for reasons of efficiency. The diamonds are based on capacity at 300 hours per month, above which they don't want to go for any extended time for reasons of employee burn-out, safety, and quality. The vertical bars represent the future workload from the Operations Plans, translated into hours, and aggregated into one number for each month. In this example, the workload is falling between the 240- and 300-hour limits for the next few months and then rises and stays above 300.

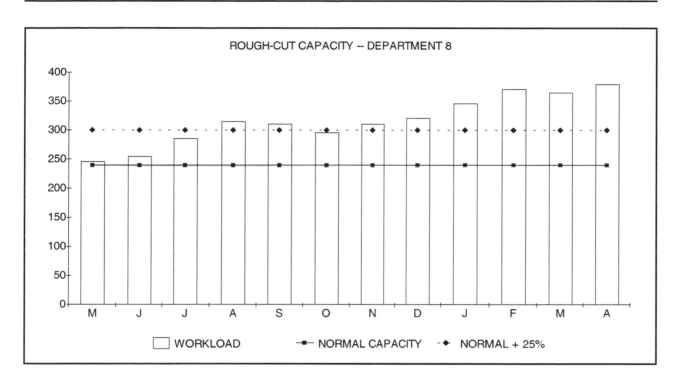

Please note: the bars — the statement of future workload — do *not* come directly from the Sales Forecast. They come from the Operations Plan, which can vary from the Sales Forecast because of backlog changes, plant shutdown, preseason production, and so on.

The decision made at the June Executive S&OP meeting was to begin interviewing for new production people in July (during plant shutdown), bring them in during August, and train them during August and September, with the goal that they'd be fully qualified and productive by October.

Try to keep your Supply Planning process simple and uncluttered with a lot of detail. Remember, we're dealing with aggregate volumes here for major groupings of production resources. We're not trying to do finite capacity loading on each machine on the plant floor, or to develop short-term schedules. Obviously, if you have a critical piece of equipment or some other resource that is typically a bottleneck, you have to keep that clearly in view for S&OP, and the best way to do that is normally with Rough-cut Capacity Planning.

Chapter 13

Bring All Families onto S&OP, Adding Supply Planning, Financial Planning, and New Products

Once you've successfully done one or two families in the S&OP pilot, it's time to start adding the other families to the process. Also, you'll be adding functions — Supply Planning, Financial Planning, and new product introductions. This time period, months four through months seven to nine, is the heart of the S&OP implementation process. It's when all of the pieces of Sales & Operations Planning come together.

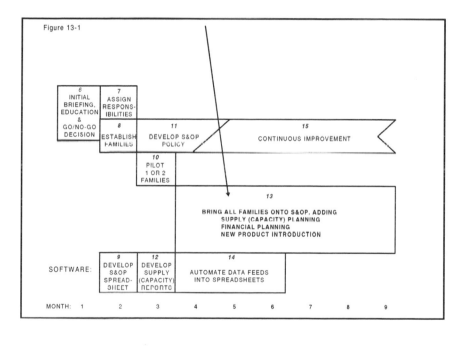

Figure 13-1

Assuming you have more than just a few families, it's best to do this in two or three groups at a time, rather than to add them all at once. Adding the remaining families, say six or nine or a dozen, all at once represents an amount of work, a level of intensity, and opportunities for error that are just not worth it.

Company S had eleven product families. They piloted with one family, added three in the second month, three in the third month and four in the fourth. Along the way, as they were adding these families, they were able to:

- Dramatically improve the process.

- Clean up their spreadsheet format.

- Add Supply (Capacity) Planning.

- Add Financial Planning.

- Add planning for New Products.

- Tie the detail to the summary.

- Automate the data feeds into their spreadsheets.

Before you start this phase, decide which families you're going to cut-over onto S&OP in which months. Then add that detailed cut-over sequence into your overall project schedule.

Add Supply (Capacity) Planning

If you're an aligned company, one where the resources match up very closely with the product families, then you're adding the Supply Planning process as you bring up the various product families. As we saw in chapter 12, you can display the capacity picture right on the S&OP spreadsheets.

If, however, you're like most companies and are in a matrix mode with families and resources, then there's a bit of a tricky timing element here. Here's the rub: S&OP can't help you evaluate the workload on a given resource until you have S&OP planning on all of the product families serviced by that resource.

For example, Company S had a matrix arrangement regarding product families and resources. In their pilot, they weren't able to do much rigorous capacity evaluation because the pilot family was made in departments that serviced other families. (This is why I said earlier that it's best to pick a pilot family that generally hasn't been having capacity problems.) However, during the next month, they added three product families that took all of the output from two of their major production departments. At that point, they were able to start up the Supply Planning part of the process because they had a full picture of the future production requirements for those departments. And, of course, as other families were added, they got a more and more complete picture of the overall supply side of their business and were able to do a first-rate job of identifying capacity bottlenecks early enough to take corrective action.

So if you're a matrix company, set your cut-over schedule for product families with an eye towards the supply side. Bring the families onto S&OP in a sequence that enables Rough-cut Capacity Planning to work sooner rather than later.

Add Financial Planning

The first steps here involve merely dollarizing some of the unit data on the spreadsheet — typically the rolling 12–18 months forecast and the sales projection for the current fiscal year. It's also very helpful to show the Business Plan's dollar number for that family. In that way, the S&OP number (latest call for the fiscal year, i.e. fiscal year-to-date actuals plus forecast for the balance of the year) can be readily compared with the Business Plan number for that family. Some companies show a percentage — S&OP's fiscal year projection versus the Business Plan — and that can be very helpful in quickly identifying where the big problems are.

Actually, it's possible to get a start at this during the pilot phase because it's not that big a deal. However, since it's usually quite a push to get that first pilot family's unit numbers put together, most companies wait until the following month to get started on the dollars.

Adding gross margin data can be helpful. Simply display the YTD margin percentage or a more robust projection of gross margin dollars for the fiscal year. You can use the same format as the latest sales call for the fiscal year — actual YTD plus forecast for the balance of the fiscal year. Dollarized production and inventory data is expressed in cost dollars and it is usually not a big challenge to assemble that information.

An important step in the overall financial integration is to aggregate all the product families — in dollars — into one view of the entire business, a sort of "master spreadsheet." Obviously, this can't be done completely until all of the families are on S&OP. And even then you might not have it all because of other revenue streams that are outside the array of product families. One approach in such cases that's proven helpful is to create a "Miscellaneous Family," to serve as a collector for atypical streams of income. Other companies just disregard this kind of thing and compare the total sales projection (out of S&OP) with a business plan number adjusted to exclude the miscellaneous incomes.

The total company dollar aggregation — the master spreadsheet — serves another purpose over and beyond sales and margin projections. For companies with make-to-stock families, it projects the planned levels of finished goods inventory for the total business. This can be valuable in companies whose business is highly seasonal. Frequently such companies engage in pre-season production with a corresponding build-up in finished inventories. The inventory dollars can get quite large. They can represent a significant cash commitment that should be planned for well in advance. With S&OP operating in dollar mode, this kind of information is always available on the master spreadsheet, updated each month to reflect changing conditions.

Once the master spreadsheet is available, it can be used in a somewhat similar fashion as the product family spreadsheets, particularly as regards performance to plan. Actual financial results can be compared with the plan for those periods. Projected sales and margin dollars can be compared with the Business Plan and appropriate corrective action decided upon.

And this leads us to one of the key issues regarding S&OP and running the business. Sometimes S&OP's latest fiscal year call — actual YTD plus forecast, in dollars — does not match the Business Plan within a few percent. In that case, what should be done? Well, you could do nothing and change neither plan. Or you might change the Sales & Operations Plan, change the Business Plan, or change them both. Let's look at each option, starting with the first one mentioned.

Change neither. I recommend against this. To leave these two very important plans with a gap between them results in running the business with two sets of numbers: the Sales & Operations Plan is directing our ongoing activities — what we buy, what we make, what we sell — down one path; while the Business Plan — representing our commitment to the corporate office, the board of directors, the stockholders — is saying something else.

This can create confusion, lack of control, a diminishing of the perceived importance of both plans, and a greater risk of not hitting the Business Plan. Not good.

Change the Sales & Operations Plan. This is appropriate, provided that more things are changed than just the numbers on the master spreadsheet page. Let's assume that the latest S&OP call for the total company is projecting a 5 percent shortfall in revenue compared with the Business Plan. Changing that number is easy. The hard part is to determine where the additional revenue is going to come from. Which families can be stimulated to generate increased sales? Are the resources available to support that, or if not, when will they be?

This not only calls for evaluating product families and resources. It means developing specific plans to increase sales, e.g. promotions, pricing, sales force incentives, perhaps accelerating new product launches. It means changing the Sales & Operations Plans for all families affected, then tracking performance against the new plans as the months unfold, and continuing to take corrective action as indicated.

Change the Business Plan. In the abstract, this should be easy to accept. After all, the Business Plan was put together some months before the beginning of the fiscal year. It's old. Doesn't it stand to reason that when a company is some months into the fiscal year, it will have a better handle on how things are likely to go? Well, then, why are so many companies so resistant to changing the older plan to match the newer plan? Because as I said above, the Business Plan is a commitment to people up the line.

Do those folks care deeply about whether Product Family A is 4 percent below plan and Product Family B is 5 percent above? Normally no. They're interested in the bottom line, i.e. in whether the business is going to generate the revenues called out in the Business Plan. The "mix" of revenue from family to family is normally the concern of the people running the business, as long as they deliver the bottom line. So I recommend that, as a general rule, the Business Plan numbers for *individual families* should be changed to reflect how the business is going to achieve the Business Plan numbers for the total business.

All of this results in running the business with one and only one set of numbers. People who do it that way will tell you that it's a very good way to manage.

Add New Products

During this phase, it's time to get new product introductions onto the S&OP radar screen. As we said earlier, new product launch issues need to be visible in all of the S&OP steps: Demand Planning phase, Supply Planning phase, Pre-SOP meeting, and Executive S&OP meeting. What's being worked here is the impact of new product introductions on the demand picture, the supply picture, and what problems are being created as a result of the new demand and supply issues. Where practical, the impact of new product launches should be displayed on the S&OP spreadsheets both in the quantitative section of the display and in the Comments sections.

Tie the Detail to the Summary

Sales & Operations Planning deals with volume, right? But we don't ship volume out the back door; we ship mix — individual products and orders. Mix is where the rubber meets the road.

So picture this: Company Z seems to have a great S&OP process. But their master scheduling operates independently and never looks at what S&OP is saying. It's disconnected. Therefore, Company Z doesn't really have a great S&OP process after all. People may be doing a lot of good work on Sales & Operations Planning, but it doesn't mean much; it's not affecting the real world.

What's needed is to add up the detail in the Master Production Schedules. Aggregate it into product families, summarize it by months, and compare it with the Operations Plan within S&OP. The sum of the Master Schedules for all the products within a given family should equal the Operations Plan plus or minus a few percent. I recommend that the Master Scheduler prepare a concise report, at least once a month, showing the comparison between the S&OP numbers and the summed Master Schedules. This linkage helps to ensure that the decisions made in Sales & Operations Planning are being transmitted downward into the detailed schedules that affect what happens on the receiving dock, the plant floor, and the shipping dock.

Good S&OP users apply the same approach to the demand side. They tally up the individual forecasts for products into product family totals and compare them with the aggregate Sales Forecasts in S&OP. This can be particularly important for companies whose aggregate forecasts are made at that aggregate level and not built up from the detail.

Chapter 14

Automate Feeds into
the S&OP Spreadsheets

Some companies are fortunate; they have all of the data they need for S&OP readily available and readily transportable into spreadsheets. If your company is a member of that happy minority, you can skip this chapter and not miss much. On the other hand, if your company isn't that fortunate, you'll need to get the data you need into the spreadsheets easily and routinely.

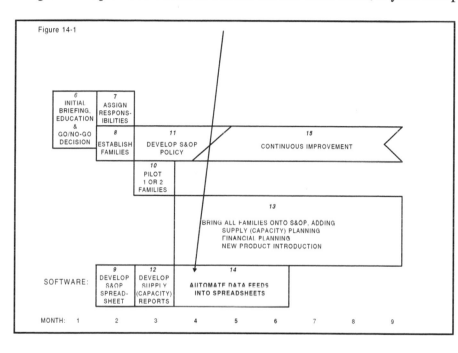

Figure 14-1

Most companies in the less fortunate category start the pilot by simply key-entering the necessary numbers directly into their spreadsheets. The reason is that frequently there will be a delay for the folks in Information Systems to automate the feeds, and so they take the line of least resistance and do manual data entry themselves. This has the benefit of not delaying the pilot — and hence the overall implementation — and helps to get people more familiar with the spreadsheet, understand what the numbers really mean, and identify shortcomings in the data.

However, if you stay on this path for too long, the data-entry job becomes onerous as more and more families and subfamilies are added to S&OP. It's also error-prone, and it's inefficient because the folks doing the keying usually don't have "data entry" in their job descriptions. They already have full-time jobs.

Therefore, it's very important that this task be taken care of early in the implementation. My advice is to start looking at this issue as soon as you decide to implement S&OP. Do you have a problem here? If so, how soon can it be taken care of? Ideally this capability would be taken care of before or during the month of the pilot so that the subsequent months can use the automated process.

I've seen implementations get delayed because of this problem, and that's not good. Delays put the entire implementation at risk: no progress means decreased enthusiasm, which in turn means a greater chance that senior management will tune out. And when those folks tune out, the project will probably die.

Some of you are probably thinking, "What's the big deal? This is not a terribly difficult or time-consuming task. How do some companies get behind the eight ball on it?" The answer is priority.

Many IS departments have large backlogs of work (owing, no doubt, to an excess of demand for their services over the available supply). The next job that comes into the department typically goes to the back of the queue, slowly works its way up the priority ladder, and — after a number of months — gets addressed and completed.

That won't work for what we're trying to do here. Manually entering increasing amounts of data into the S&OP spreadsheets can result in errors, frustration, and a slower rate of progress as more and more families are added. One of the keys in a successful implementation is to increase both the quantity and quality of the data: more families need to be added quickly, and thus the data itself must get more accurate and more complete at the same time. Key-entering data for a half dozen or more product families and perhaps several dozen subfamilies is not the way to get there.

My recommendation is, at the very onset of the project, to establish S&OP as a high-priority activity. Since this step is on the critical path for implementing S&OP, then it also has high priority. Get a commitment from the IS folks to complete this step early in the project. If necessary, the S&OP Executive Sponsor can be called upon to help set the priorities. This task should be completed no later than a month or so following the pilot — and since it's almost never a lot of work, there's no good reason why it shouldn't be.

Chapter 15

Continuous Improvement

There are two main pieces to this important topic: internal and external. "Internal" means within the S&OP process itself, and "external" refers to processes outside of S&OP — other processes that affect customer service, finished goods inventories, customer lead times, et cetera.

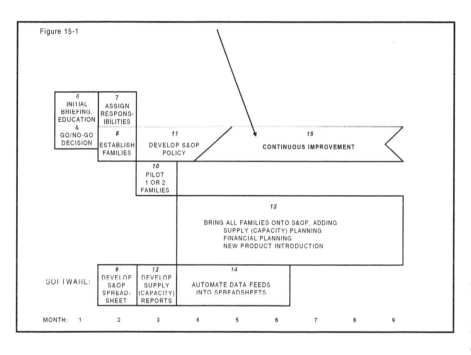

Figure 15-1

Internal Improvement — Critique of the Executive S&OP Meeting

"Internal improvement" refers to improvement within Sales & Operations Planning itself. Two tools exist to help companies make continuous improvements in their S&OP processes, one of which we've already seen. It's the last item on the agenda of the Executive S&OP meeting: critique of the meeting. If you do this each month, I can almost guarantee that you'll be delighted with how much better the meetings become. It doesn't need to take a lot of time, normally five or ten minutes.

One good way to conduct this critique is to simply go around the room and ask each person to give his or her reaction to the meeting, pointing out areas for improvement. I've observed a few companies do the critique very effectively by each person's assigning a numerical grade to the meeting on a scale of 1 to 10 and stating the reason for that grade. Some companies make it a practice to let the president go last and to make the concluding remarks.

However you do it, the critiques should not be viewed as bad news but rather as opportunities for improvement. As such, they should be documented in the meeting minutes and addressed prior to the next meeting.

Internal Improvement — The S&OP Effectiveness Checklist

The checklist is the second element in continuously improving the S&OP process, and it is shown in full at the end of this chapter. As you can see, it contains a series of twenty-five items that can be answered with a "yes," a "partial," or a "no." It contains instructions for scoring the responses and evaluating how well the S&OP process is being used.

I recommend that you begin using the checklist during the month following the pilot, i.e. during month three. It's unlikely that you'll score very high on that first evaluation, but that's okay. Working the checklist at this early stage will point out the areas where you're doing well, and that's good feedback. It will also point out what remains to be done, which at this early stage will be quite a bit. Your main focus should be on completing the items on the project schedule, so the checklist results should be viewed primarily as supporting information to the schedule. In some cases, I've seen people modify the project schedule based on results of the checklist. As you go forward into months four and beyond, the project schedule will play a diminishing role and the checklist should become more dominant in directing what needs to be done. Feel free to photocopy it.

External Improvement

S&OP's contribution to continuous improvement in other parts of the company's operations is addressed in item 12 on the checklist, which reads:

> Demand/supply strategies for each product family are formally reviewed quarterly in the Pre-SOP and S&OP meetings, with a view towards increasing customer service targets, reducing finished goods inventory targets, and reducing customer order backlog targets.

Let's say that, for one of your make-to-stock families, your target customer service level is 98 percent and your target finished goods level is fifteen days' supply. Let's say you've been hitting those targets for some months now. So what should be done?

What should *not* be done is to do nothing. The spirit of continuous improvement should lead the company to target either an increase in customer service, a reduction in finished goods, or possibly both. So how should that be done?

Well, it's usually not enough to simply change the numbers on the page. What needs to be done is to get into the underlying processes and to start asking some questions:

- Why do we need fifteen days of inventory to give 98 percent customer service?

- What process changes could we make to cut the inventory down to twelve days and not hurt customer service?

- What if we reduced the changeover time on the equipment that makes the product for this family? That means we could make shorter production runs, our inventory would go down, and customer service wouldn't drop and might even increase.

- Could we do anything to reduce the forecast error on the items in this family? If so, we'd need less safety stock and could give the same or better customer service.

- How about cutting manufacturing and purchasing lead times? If we could do that, we'd become more flexible and that means giving higher customer service with equal or lower inventories.

Another opportunity here concerns time fences. Let's say that Company Y has the following time fence set at the end of month three: no production rate changes beyond +10 percent and −20 percent. When was that last changed? If it's been that way ever since they started on Sales & Operations Planning, it seems to me that they're falling down on the continuous improvement side of the process. I recommend that Operations work hard at becoming more flexible so that Company Y can give better customer service, reduce inventories, and improve its financial picture. When they become more flexible, that should be reflected in their time fences.

What I'm getting at is that there's a lot more to continuous improvement than changing the numbers on a piece of paper. Rather, the key is to improve underlying processes. The important contribution of Sales & Operations Planning here is that it raises the visibility of process improvements to the top management team and expresses them in terms that are easy for them to understand: customer service, customer lead times, and finished goods inventory investment.

THE S&OP EFFECTIVENESS CHECKLIST

COMPANY/DIVISION: _____ **DATE:** _____

1. Sales & Operations Planning is a monthly process involving both middle management and top management, including the president (general manager, COO). yes   partial   no

2. The monthly S&OP cycle consists of a Demand Planning phase, a Supply Planning phase, a Pre-SOP meeting, and an Executive S&OP meeting that includes the president. yes   partial   no

3. A written Sales & Operations Planning policy details the participants, responsibilities, timing, and objectives of each step in the process. yes   partial   no

4. Meeting dates for the Pre-SOP and Executive S&OP meetings are scheduled well into the future, to maximize attendance. yes   partial   no

5. The Executive S&OP meeting is rescheduled if the president is unable to attend. Other participants who cannot attend a given meeting are represented by their designated alternates, who are empowered to participate in the decision-making process. yes   partial   no

6. A written agenda is issued at least two work days before each Executive S&OP meeting, highlighting major decisions that need to be made at that meeting. yes   partial   no

7. The Executive S&OP meeting operates at an aggregate, family level and rarely focuses on individual items. yes   partial   no

8. The number of product families is in the range of 5 to 15. Subfamilies are used in the Pre-SOP steps where appropriate. yes   partial   no

9. Sales & Marketing "own" the Sales Forecast. They understand and accept their responsibility: to provide forecasts that are reasoned, reasonable, reviewed at least monthly, and reflect the total demand. yes   partial   no

10. Operations "owns" the Operations Plan. They understand and accept their responsibility: to develop plans that support the Sales Forecast, meet the demand/supply strategies, and are cost-effective for production. yes   partial   no

11. Customer service performance measures (on-time and complete shipments) are reviewed at each Pre-SOP and Executive S&OP meeting. yes   partial   no

12. Demand/supply strategies for each product family are formally reviewed quarterly in the Pre-SOP and Executive S&OP meetings with a view towards increasing customer service targets, reducing finished goods inventory targets, and reducing customer order backlog targets. yes   partial   no

13. The S&OP process covers all important parts of the business and extends at least twelve months into the future. yes   partial   no

14. The S&OP spreadsheet contains all key information on one page: past performance to plan, customer service statistics, and future forecasts and operations plans. yes   partial   no

15. In addition to quantitative information, the S&OP spreadsheet also shows qualitative, verbal information in the form of assumptions and issues that need to be recognized.　　　　yes　partial　no

16. To identify plant overload/underload problems, separate capacity displays are used where there is not a one-for-one match between product families and production resources.　　　　yes　partial　no

17. New product development issues that may impact the demand/supply relationship are a permanent agenda item for both the Pre-SOP and Executive S&OP meetings.　　　　yes　partial　no

18. The Master Production Schedule is compared, at least monthly, with the Operations Plan in S&OP to ensure that the Master Schedule is set at the levels authorized in the Executive S&OP meeting.　　　　yes　partial　no

19. Sales & Operations Planning is a decision-making process. The Pre-SOP Team decides what recommendations to make to the executive group, and the Executive S&OP Team decides to accept those recommendations or adopt an alternative.　　　　yes　partial　no

20. Members of the Finance & Accounting function play an important role in both the Pre-SOP phases and in the Executive S&OP meeting itself to ensure that the plans have financial validity.　　　　yes　partial　no

21. In the Executive S&OP meeting, dollarized versions of the Sales & Operations Plan are compared with the Business Plan (annual budget, operating plan). As appropriate, the Business Plan is updated to reflect the new realities identified in S&OP.　　　　yes　partial　no

22. In the spirit of continuous improvement, a brief critique of the Executive S&OP meeting is held before the end of each meeting. Feedback is solicited from all participants.　　　　yes　partial　no

23. Minutes of the S&OP meeting detailing all decisions made are distributed within two work days after the meeting.　　　　yes　partial　no

24. The Sales & Operations Planning process has become the framework for decision-making regarding all major demand/supply issues.　　　　yes　partial　no

25. Improvement has been achieved in at least four of the following six performance areas: higher customer service, lower customer order backlogs, shorter customer lead times, higher turnover of the finished goods inventory, reduced unplanned overtime, lower hiring and lay-off costs.　　　　yes　partial　no

---

SCORING:　　YES = 1　　PARTIAL = ½　　NO = 0

					23 – 25:	Excellent
_____	+	_____ /2	=	_____	>>>	20 – 22: Good
# YES		# PARTIAL		TOTAL SCORE		17 – 19: Fair
						less than 17: Poor

Chapter 16

Special Situations

No two companies are exactly alike obviously, and thus Sales & Operations Planning won't look exactly the same from one company to another.

So far in this handbook, we've laid out the generic path to follow for a successful S&OP implementation. Now it's time to look at some special challenges that companies face. It's highly unlikely that you'll be confronted with all of them, or even most of them. However chances are good that you'll have to grapple with at least one of them.

Multiple Sales/Marketing Units

When a given producing division is providing product to other business units, it needs processes to ensure that all demands are recognized. The solution often centers around determining who the immediate customers are.

Roger was the general manager of Division P. A majority of his production went to other divisions in the corporation. Roger questioned his division's ability to use S&OP effectively because they had no direct contact with the other divisions' customers. Roger said that there was no way they could do a good job of Demand Planning because they couldn't get to the customers.

His view changed when he started to look upon the other divisions as the customers. His job performance would be judged in part on how well his division was able to service these "internal customers." The better job he did, the happier his internal customers would be, and the more highly Roger's division would be regarded.

Division P's approach to Demand Planning for the sister divisions was to work closely with their people in projecting future demand, to get the best forecast numbers they possibly could. They visited these divisions once a month and were in contact with them between visits. Were the resulting forecasts highly accurate? Of course not. Were they better than before? Absolutely. And they got even better over time, as the other divisions came to appreciate the process and the fact that they were getting better customer service than ever before.

Multiple Plants

Frequently companies have more than one plant, and of course S&OP has to reflect that. Naturally, companies with aligned resources have an easier time of it and here's an example.

Company A has plants in Pennsylvania, Illinois, Texas, and California. Since Company A has aligned resources, its plants match up closely with the product families. Thus it was able to set up subfamilies by plant. For example, Product Family 9 is produced both in Pennsylvania and Texas, so the company established two subfamilies: Product Subfamily 9 (Pennsylvania), and Product Subfamily 9 (Texas).

These subfamilies are forecasted and planned individually in the Demand, Supply, and Pre-SOP steps. For the Executive S&OP meeting, the main focus is on the total Product Family 9. However, there are times when it's necessary to look at a subfamily, for instance when there's a serious overload in one of the plants, say Pennsylvania. Scenarios could then include:

- Transferring some production from Pennsylvania to Texas, at some percentage increase in freight costs.

- Adding a third shift in Pennsylvania, at some percentage increase in overhead at that plant.

- Offloading some other volume from Pennsylvania to Illinois, with only a minor freight cost penalty but requiring some new equipment in Illinois, at a capital expenditure that is not in the current year's capital budget.

For matrix, nonaligned arrangements, the standard Rough-cut Capacity Planning approach works fine. Company L has an injection molding plant in Oklahoma and one in Ohio. Its forecasting needs to be done at a level of detail that allows demand to be assigned to the plants on the proper basis. In general, demand for Company L's products from east of the Mississippi River goes to the Ohio plant and the rest to Oklahoma.

Having multiple plants usually means having remote plants, and having that means that key people from each plant will take part in Sales & Operations Planning. Normally it's not considered practical to have these folks travel into headquarters each month for S&OP, nor — in this day of teleconferencing and video conferencing — is it necessary. What can be helpful is to bring each one of these players into headquarters once during the early phases of implementation, perhaps when their respective plants are being added to the process. Some companies then bring the appropriate people into headquarters for an S&OP meeting once a year, for a bit of refresher, and for some face-to-face contact with people whom they normally don't see.

Combination Families:
Make-to-Order and Make-to-Stock

Some families contain both make-to-order and make-to-stock products. It can be useful to break out the product family into two subfamilies: one for make-to-order and the other for make-to-stock. These subfamilies are reviewed separately during the Demand, Supply, and Pre-SOP steps.

Then for the Executive S&OP meeting, combine them onto one spreadsheet for the total family. This spreadsheet might have to be a bit different. It would almost certainly have to show both an inventory section and an order backlog section, so that these competitive variables can be visible, and it may also be desirable to break out the demand separately into the make-to-stock and make-to-order components.

Assemble-to-Order, Build-to-Order, and
Finish-to-Order Families

Products in these categories, also called "make-to-demand," are finished to customer order out of stocked components. As such they lie somewhere between a pure make-to-order product and one that's make-to-stock.

Most often, backlogs of such products can be measured in only a few days. Their finished inventory ranges from zero to occasionally a day or two of supply, reflecting perhaps the staging of large orders. Thus both the target backlog and target finished inventory can be near zero. There can be some significant inventory in the system, however, typically at the stage of production right before the finishing operation.

Company N, for example, makes an assembled product to customer order out of stocked modules. Their products are mechanical, not electronic, but conceptually the approach is very similar to Dell Computer's: the customers order a specific configuration from a "menu" of standard options. Company N has learned that the amount of module inventory must be about five days' supply to account for variations in the actual usage versus forecast. One can look upon this as safety stock, not dissimilar from the target finished goods inventory for a purely make-to-stock product family.

It's important that Company N plan for this five-day supply, because without it they would be unable to keep the backlog and finished goods inventory near zero. On their S&OP spreadsheets, they show the amount of module inventory in aggregate units and also the number of days' supply; that enables them to easily reflect changes in forecasted sales volume to final assembly workload and to drive the module inventory to the correct level.

Combination Families: Manufactured and Outsourced

Company D is in the container business. For one of its families, the product is sourced internally from one of its thirteen plants, from domestic suppliers, and from suppliers in Asia.

In this case, the product family is broken up into three subfamilies by source. The subfamilies are reviewed during the Demand, Supply, and Pre-SOP steps. The Executive S&OP meeting looks at the family spreadsheet — which in this case shows separate supply information for each of the three different sources.

Field Inventories

Company B sells through distributors, and also through manufacturers' representatives who stock the product. The inventory at these stocking reps is on consignment; Company B owns it until it's sold. The S&OP process, to be effective, must have visibility into that inventory. Without it, a key component of the supply side of the demand/supply equation is missing. Such a lack would result in making less-effective decisions.

The inventory of Company B's products at the distributors is *not* on consignment; the distributors own it. However, shouldn't Company B be looking at the distributors' inventories of their products, even though that inventory is not owned by Company B? I certainly think so. Actually, this piece of inventory is more important than what's at the stocking reps, even though Company B doesn't own it. Why? Because it's a lot bigger number; there's a lot more inventory at the distributors.

In short, to effectively balance supply with demand, you need to see the finished inventories in the field regardless of who owns them.

S&OP for Nonphysical Products

Company M is in the aerospace business. One of its groups makes highly engineered widgets for things that fly fast: spacecraft, satellites, and missiles, among other things. Within the Systems Group, there are several separate divisions that produce and sell products. However, the *design* of the products is done centrally within the Group.

Product Design and Development performs work for the producing divisions, but it also does advanced engineering projects for NASA and others. There is, therefore, a wide variety of demands placed on this department. Product Design and Development also has a finite supply of engineering talent, which is not easy to increase in the short run.

Might this be a logical application for Sales & Operations Planning, even though there are no physical products involved?

Well, the group vice president had the same idea. Following successful implementations of S&OP in the product divisions, he asked the design and development folks to consider the process. They did consider it, and they adopted it, and they adapted it to their particular operation. Some of the information displayed at their meetings is a bit different, but the process itself is virtually identical to that used in the divisions that make and sell the product.

In other words, nowhere is it written that you must be making physical products in order to take advantage of this powerful tool. If you have problems balancing demand for nonphysical outputs with supply, S&OP might be a big help.

Chapter 17

What's Coming

A few words about the future are in order.

On the one hand, I've learned that making predictions is a very iffy business. Some of my predictions have been amazingly accurate — right on the mark. Unfortunately, they're in a distinct minority. I might have done better with a dart board.

But it's important to think about what lies ahead, if for no other reason than to try to get ready for it. As I hope I've shown, S&OP is so helpful precisely because it is a window into the (short- to medium-run) future. So here are some of my hopes (not predictions, mind you) for the continued evolution and growth of Sales & Operations Planning:

- S&OP will continue to be adopted by more and more businesses, and the rate of adoption will accelerate. One reason this should happen is that S&OP works, and word gets around. Another is that executives who use it become true believers in the process. As they move from one division to another, or from one company to another, they take S&OP with them.

- S&OP is collaborative and cross-functional. It stands in sharp contrast to its predecessor, the process called Production Planning, which is sequential and stand-alone. As more companies become aware of the benefits of cross-functional team processes, S&OP will look increasingly attractive.

- As Supply Chain Management becomes more widely accepted, S&OP will be viewed as essential in order to harmonize the entire supply chain.

- As business becomes increasingly international, the use of Sales & Operations Planning will become "globalized" in those companies operating globally. Operating on a truly global basis — as opposed to doing business worldwide by region — can be far more challenging and S&OP can help with that, a lot.

- More software vendors will offer an "S&OP module" as part of their ERP suites, and that software will improve in quality from today's offerings. Packaged S&OP software will raise awareness and trigger companies to get into it.

Last, please bear with me for just a moment, while I engage in what may seem like some major blue-sky prognosticating. Imagine that you've successfully implemented Sales & Operations Planning in your company. Your top management team is meeting once a month to authorize sales and operations plans that will harmonize demand and supply and to integrate those plans with the financials. In an Executive S&OP meeting, one of the attendees — the president or perhaps the CFO — raises a question: *If we can pull up the new product launch by six weeks, we're sure we can beat the competition to the market. Can we do it? If so, what other products might be affected? Would we have enough raw material and capacity to do that?*

You're projecting the S&OP display for this product family onto a large screen from your PC, which contains the ERP data base for the entire company. You ask for a brief time-out while you run the simulation using your advanced planning system (APS) software. Within no more than a few minutes, you have answers: Plan A is feasible but will negatively affect product 123 because of raw material availability problems; Plan B is feasible but will impact products 234 and 345 slightly; and Plan C will have the least total cost but will cause serious stockouts across much of the product line, because of capacity constraints in Fabrication. Armed with these facts, the Executive S&OP Team is well equipped to make the right decision. They'll most likely select Plan B: it's feasible; it has only slight negative impact; and it accelerates the new product launch.

The phrase "top management war room" comes to mind. I'm looking forward to the day when this type of capability is widespread: Sales & Operations Planning linked with APS/simulation software running at the speed of light — supporting major demand/supply decisions with facts, not guesses — in a top management setting. That is where I'd like to see S&OP by the year 2010.

I do hope this handbook proves helpful to you. Good luck and Godspeed.

Appendix A

Sales & Operations Planning
Generalized Implementation Plan

Please note: This is a generalized plan and is meant to be used to tailor the individual company plan. As such, some tasks may not be necessary and can be dropped, while other tasks may need to be added. It is designed to show the planned start and completion dates for each step and contains room for amplifying comments. Overall this plan follows the Implementation Path diagram.

TASK	PERSON(S) RESPONSIBLE	START PLAN	START ACTUAL	COMPLETE PLAN	COMPLETE ACTUAL	COMMENTS
010 Conduct Initial Briefing						
020 Conduct Education Day						
030 Make Go/No-go Decision						
040 Determine Team Members:						
Demand Planning Team						
Supply Planning Team						
Pre-SOP Team						
Executive S&OP Team						
Exec Champion/Sponsor						
S&OP Process Owner						
Spreadsheet Developer						
Consulting Support						
050 Dates Set for Next 12 S&OP Meetings						
060 Dates Set for Next 12 Pre-SOP Meetings						
070 Product Families Identified						
080 Product Units of Measure Defined						

TASK	PERSON(S) RESPONSIBLE	START PLAN ACTUAL	COMPLETE PLAN ACTUAL	COMMENTS
090 Resources Identified				
100 Capacity Units of Measure Defined				
110 Planning Horizon Set				
120 Pilot Family Selected				
130 Demand/Supply Strategies Set for Pilot Family				
140 S&OP Spreadsheet Format Designed				
150 S&OP Spreadsheet Programmed				
160 First Demand Planning Process Completed				
170 First Supply Planning Process Completed				
180 First Pre-SOP Meeting Conducted				
190 First S&OP Meeting Conducted				
200 Families to Be Added in Second Set of Meetings Identified				
210 Draft of S&OP Policy Developed and Circulated				
220 Capacity Planning Display Designed				
230 Capacity Planning Display Programmed				
240 Forecast Aggregation/ Disaggregation Techniques Developed				

TASK	PERSON(S) RESPONSIBLE	START PLAN ACTUAL	COMPLETE PLAN ACTUAL	COMMENTS
250 Sales and Forecast Feeds to S&OP Spreadsheet Automated				
260 Actual and Planned Production Feeds to S&OP Spreadsheet Automated				
270 Actual Inventory/Backlog Feeds to S&OP Spreadsheet Automated				
280 Demand/Supply Strategies Set for All Families				
290 Second Pre-SOP Meeting Conducted				
300 Second S&OP Meeting Conducted				
310 Begin Formal Capacity Evaluation within the S&OP Process				
320 Begin to Display Financial Numbers and Tie to Business Plan				
330 Begin New Product Introduction Evaluation				
340 Begin to Tie Operations Plan to Master Production Schedule				
350 Other Significant Issues Added to S&OP Agenda: Obsolescence Special Projects Others				

TASK	PERSON(S) RESPONSIBLE	START PLAN ACTUAL	COMPLETE PLAN ACTUAL	COMMENTS
360 Third Pre-SOP Meeting Conducted				
370 Third Executive S&OP Meeting Conducted				
380 Sales & Operations Planning Policy Approved by Executive S&OP Team				
390 Fourth Pre-SOP Meeting Conducted				
400 Fourth Executive S&OP Meeting Conducted				
410 Formalize Business Plan Review within S&OP Meeting				
420 Evaluate Other Routinely Held Meetings for Discontinuance or Integration with Sales & Operations Planning Meetings				
430 Test the S&OP Process against S&OP Checklist				
440 All Product Families and Resources Covered by S&OP				
450 Improve and Refine the Total S&OP Process				
460 Integrate S&OP with Other Continuous Improvement Processes				

Appendix B

Resource Material

Books

Orchestrating Success: Improve Control of the Business with Sales & Operations Planning, by Richard C. Ling and Walter E. Goddard. New York: John Wylie & Sons, Inc., 1988.

The Marketing Edge: The New Leadership Role of Sales & Marketing in Manufacturing, by George E. Palmatier and Joseph S. Shull. New York: John Wylie & Sons, Inc., 1989.

Articles

"Drive the Business with Sales & Operations Planning" by Arne Brander. *APICS — The Performance Advantage,* August 1998, pp. 48-51.

"The S&OP Process — An Old Idea Gaining New Interest and Praise" by Donald J. Sheldon. *Mid-Range ERP,* January-February 1998.

"Sales & Operations Planning — Report from the Field" by Tom Wallace. *APICS — The Performance Advantage,* February 1997, pp 34-38.

"Game Planning," by David Rucinski. *Production and Inventory Management Journal,* First Quarter, 1982, pp 63-68.

Papers

"Beyond Sales & Operations Planning: An Integrated Global Business Planning Process," by Richard C. Ling and Andy Coldrick. In *38th International Conference Proceedings,* pp.191–95. Falls Church, Va.: APICS, 1995.

"Sales & Operations Planning – A Fundamental That Still Works," by Robert A. Stahl. In *International Conference Proceedings,* pp. 97–100. Alexandria, Va.: APICS 1999.

"Does Your Company Need a Sales & Operations Planning Tune-Up?" by John J. Civerolo. In *36th International Conference Proceedings,* pp. 288–90. Falls Church, Va.: APICS, 1993.

"Getting Results with Sales & Operations Planning," by John V. Briggs and William J. Jones. In *31st Annual International Conference Proceedings,* pp. 91–95. Falls Church, Va.: APICS, 1988.

"The Role of S&OP and Demand Management in EDI and ECR," by Daphne Perry and George Palmatier. In *37th International Conference Proceedings,* pp. 462–67. Falls Church, Va.: APICS, 1994.

"Sales & Operations Planning: The Bridge between Sales and Operations," by Pete Liberante and Don J. Nading. In *Process Industries Symposium Proceedings,* pp. 89–91. Falls Church, Va.: APICS, 1991.

"Sales & Operations Planning as a Competitive Weapon: A Case Study," by George Palmatier. In *Aerospace & Defense Symposium Proceedings,* pp. 109–13. Falls Church, Va.: APICS, 1992.

"Sales & Operations Planning: Our Story," by William Hemmings and Rebecca Kennedy. In *Process Industries Symposium Proceedings,* pp. 36–41. Falls Church, Va.: APICS, 1993.

"Sales & Operations Planning: The Integrator of the Business Planning Process," by Richard C. Ling. In *1998 International Conference Proceedings,* pp. 177–80. Falls Church, Va.: APICS, 1998.

"A Vision Becomes Reality: The Eight Critical Steps to Successful Implementation of Sales & Operations Planning," by James Correll and Rory MacDowell. In *International Conference Proceedings,* pp. 92-95. Falls Church, Va.: APICS, 1997.

Appendix C

Glossary

Author's note: Wherever practical, I've tried to use existing definitions from the ninth edition of the APICS Dictionary. Those have been noted (APICS). The definitions I've supplied myself are in italics.*

Aligned Resources — *Resources that match up very closely with the product families. For example, all of the production for Family A is done in Department 1 and Department 1 makes no product for any other family; similarly for Family B and Department 2, and so on. Determining future capacity requirements for aligned resources is simpler than for matrix resources. See* **Matrix Resources.**

Assemble-to-Order — A production environment where a good or service can be assembled after receipt of a customer's order. The key components (bulk, semifinished, intermediate, subassembly, fabricated, purchased, packaging, etc.) used in the assembly or finishing process are planned and possibly stocked in anticipation of a customer order. Receipt of an order initiates assembly of the customized product. This strategy is useful where a large number of end products (based on the selection of options and accessories) can be assembled from common components. (APICS)

Build-to-Order — *Term popularized by Dell Computer which means much the same thing as* **Assemble-to-Order.**

Business Plan — 1) A statement of long-range strategy and revenue, cost, and profit objectives usually accompanied by budgets, a projected balance sheet, and a cash flow (source and application of funds) statement. A business plan is usually stated in terms of dollars and grouped by product family. The business plan, the sales and operations plan, and the production plan, although frequently stated in different terms, should agree with each other.... 2) A document consisting of the business details (organization, strategy, financing tactics) prepared by an entrepreneur to plan for a new business. (APICS)

Capacity Planning — *The process of determining how much capacity will be required to produce in the future. Capacity planning can occur at an aggregate level (see* **Rough-cut Capacity Planning***) or at a detailed level. Tools employed for the latter include the traditional Capacity*

---

*James F. Cox III and John H. Blackstone Jr., eds., *APICS Dictionary,* ninth edition (Falls Church, Virginia: APICS, 1998). Terms and definitions used with permission.

Requirements Planning process and the newer Finite Capacity Planning/Scheduling, which not only recognize specific overloads but make recommendations for overcoming them.

Demand Management — The function of recognizing all demands for goods and services to support the marketplace. It involves doing what is required to help make the demand happen and prioritizing demand when supply is lacking. Proper demand management facilitates the planning and use of resources for profitable business results. It encompasses the activities of forecasting, order entry, order promising, and determining branch warehouse requirements, interplant orders, and service parts requirements. (APICS)

Demand Manager — *A job function charged with coordinating the demand management process. Frequently the demand manager will operate the statistical forecasting system and work closely with other marketing and sales people in the Demand Planning phase of S&OP. Other activities for the demand manager might include making decisions regarding abnormal demand, working closely with the master scheduler on product availability issues, and being a key player in other aspects of the monthly Sales & Operations Planning process. This may or may not be a full-time position.*

Demand Plan — *The Sales Plan (forecast) and other anticipated demands such as interplant, export, and samples. See:* **Sales Plan**.

Demand/Supply Strategies — *A statement for each product family that defines how the company "meets the customer" with that product, its objectives in terms of customer service levels, and targets for finished inventory or order backlog levels. For example, Family A is make-to-stock (i.e. it is shipped to customers from finished goods inventory), its target line fill is 99.5 percent, and its target finished inventory level is ten days' supply.*

Enterprise Resources Planning (ERP) System — 1) An accounting-oriented information system for identifying and planning the enterprise-wide resources needed to take, make, ship, and account for customer orders. An ERP system differs from the typical MRP II system in technical requirements such as graphical user interface, relational database, use of fourth-generation language, and computer-assisted software engineering tools in development, client/server architecture, and open-system portability. 2) More generally, a method for the effective planning and control of all resources needed to take, make, ship, and account for customer orders in a manufacturing, distribution, or service company. (APICS)

Executive S&OP Meeting — *The culminating step in the monthly Sales & Operations Planning cycle. It is a decision-making meeting, attended by the president/general manager, his or her staff, and other key individuals.*

Family — *See:* **Product Family.**

Financial Interface — *A process of tying financial information and operating information together. It is the process by which businesses are able to operate with one and only one set of numbers, rather than using data in operational functions that differ from that used in the financial side of the business.*

Finish-to-Order — *See:* **Assemble-to-Order.**

Forecast — An estimate of future demand. A forecast can be determined by mathematical means using historical data, it can be created subjectively by using estimates from informal sources, or it can represent a combination of both techniques. (APICS)

Line Fill Rate — *The percentage of lines (individual line items on customer orders) shipped on time and complete as opposed to the total number of lines ordered.*

Make-to-Order — A production environment where a good or service can be made after receipt of a customer's order. The final product is usually a combination of standard items and items custom-designed to meet the special needs of the customer. Where options or accessories are stocked before customer orders arrive, the term **assemble-to-order** is frequently used. See: **Assemble-to-Order, Make-to-Stock.** (APICS)

Make-to-Stock — A production environment where products can be and usually are finished before receipt of a customer order. Customer orders are typically filled from existing stocks, and production orders are used to replenish those stocks. See: **Assemble-to-Order, Make-to-Order.** (APICS)

Manufacturing Resource Planning (MRP II) — A method for the effective planning of all resources of a manufacturing company. Ideally, it addresses operational planning in units, financial planning in dollars, and has a simulation capability to answer "what if " questions. It is made up of a variety of functions, each linked together: business planning, sales and operations planning, production planning, master production scheduling, material requirements planning, capacity requirements planning, and the execution support systems for capacity and material. Output from these systems is integrated with financial reports such as the business plan, purchase commitment report, shipping budget, and inventory projections in dollars.... (APICS)

Master Production Schedule (MPS) — 1) The anticipated build schedule for those items assigned to the master scheduler. The master scheduler maintains this schedule, and in turn, it becomes a set of planning numbers that drives material requirements planning. It represents what the company plans to produce expressed in specific configurations, quantities, and dates. The master production schedule is not a sales forecast that represents a statement of demand. The master production schedule must take into account the forecast, the production plan, and other important considerations such as backlog, availability of material, availability of capacity, and management policies and goals. Syn: **master schedule.** 2) The result of the master scheduling process. The master schedule is a presentation of demand, forecast, backlog, the MPS, the projected on-hand inventory, and the available-to-promise quantity. (APICS)

Master Schedule — *See:* **Master Production Schedule.**

Matrix Resources — *Resources that do not match up with the product families. For example, Department 1 makes products in Families A, C, D, and G. Determining future capacity requirements for matrix resources is somewhat more complex than for aligned resources. See:* **Aligned Resources.**

Mix — *The details. Individual products, customer orders, pieces of equipment — as opposed to aggregate groupings. See:* **Volume.**

Operations Plan — *The agreed-upon rates and volumes of production or procurement to support the Sales Plan (Demand Plan, Sales Forecast) and to reach the inventory or order backlog targets. The Operations Plan, upon authorization at the Executive S&OP meeting, becomes the "marching orders" for the master scheduler, who must set the Master Production Schedule in congruence with the Operations Plan.*

Order Fill Rate — *The percentage of customer orders shipped on time and complete as opposed to the total number of orders. Order fill is a more stringent measure of customer delivery performance than line fill. For example, if only one item out of twenty on a customer order is unavailable, then that order counts for zero in the order fill calculation. The line fill percentage in this example would be 95 percent. See:* **Line Fill Rate.**

Pre-SOP Meeting — *The preliminary session prior to the Executive S&OP meeting. In it, key people from Sales and Marketing, Operations, Finance, and New Product Development come together to develop the recommendations to be made at the Executive S&OP session.*

Product Family — *The basic planning element for Sales & Operations Planning. S&OP's focus is on families and subfamilies (volume), not individual items (mix).*

Product Subfamily — *A planning element sometimes used in S&OP that provides a more detailed view than product families, but not at the extreme detail of individual products. Product Family A, for example, might contain three subfamilies — A1, A2, A3 — and each of those might contain a dozen or so individual products. See:* **Product Family.**

Production Plan — *See:* **Operations Plan.**

Resource — Anything that adds value to a good or service in its creation, production, or delivery. (APICS)

Resource Requirements Planning — *See:* **Rough-cut Capacity Planning.**

Rough-cut Capacity Planning — *The process by which the Operations Plan or the Master Production Schedule can be converted into future capacity requirements. Frequently the Operations Plan, expressed in units of product, is "translated" into standard hours of workload (which is a common unit of measure for production operations). Rough-cut Capacity Planning can be used at the departmental level, or for subsets of departments down to individual pieces of equipment or specific skill levels for production associates. This process can also be carried out for suppliers, for warehouse space, and for non-production operations such as product design and drafting.*

Sales & Operations Planning (S&OP) — *A business process that helps companies keep demand and supply in balance. It does that by focusing on aggregate volumes — product families and groups — so that mix issues — individual products and customer orders — can be handled more readily. It occurs on a monthly cycle and displays information in both units and dollars. S&OP is cross-functional, involving General Management, Sales, Operations, Finance, and Product Development. It occurs at multiple levels within the company, up to and including the executive in charge of the business unit, e.g. division president, business unit general manager, or CEO of a smaller corporation. S&OP links the company's Strategic Plans and Business Plan to its detailed processes — the order entry, master scheduling, plant scheduling, and purchasing tools it uses to run the business on a week-to-week, day-to-day, and hour-to-hour basis. Used properly, S&OP enables the* *company's managers to view the business holistically and provides them with a window into the future.*

Sales Plan — A time-phased statement of expected customer orders anticipated to be received ... for each major product family or item. It represents sales and marketing management's commitment to take all reasonable steps necessary to achieve this level of actual customer orders. The Sales Plan is a necessary input to the ... sales and operations planning process.... (APICS)

Stockkeeping Unit (SKU) — *A specific, individual product. In the more rigorous use of the term, it refers to a specific, individual product in a given location. Thus, product #1234 at the Los Angeles warehouse is a different SKU from the same product at the Chicago warehouse.*

Subfamily — *See:* **Product Subfamily**.

Supply Chain — 1) The processes from the initial raw materials to the ultimate consumption of the finished product linking across supplier-user companies. 2) The functions inside and outside a company that enable the value chain to make products and provide services to the customer. (APICS)

Supply Chain Management — The planning, organizing, and controlling of supply chain activities. (APICS)

Supply Planning — *The function of setting planned rates of production (both in-house and outsourced) to satisfy the demand plan and to meet inventory and order backlog targets. Frequently, Rough-cut Capacity Planning is used to support this.*

Time Fence — A policy or guideline established to note where various restrictions or changes in operating procedures take place. For example, changes to the master production scheduled can be accomplished easily beyond the cumulative lead time, while changes inside the cumulative lead time become increasingly more difficult to a point where changes should be resisted. Time fences can be used to define these points. (APICS)

Volume — *The big picture. Sales and production rates for aggregate groupings — product families, production departments, etc. — as opposed to individual products, customer orders, and work centers. See:* **Mix.**

Appendix D

The Difference between Production Planning and Sales & Operations Planning

Perhaps the best way to contrast Sales & Operations Planning with its predecessor, Production Planning, is to view them graphically. On the next page, please see Figure D-1, showing the Production Planning method.

Notice that the Sales Planning and Production Planning boxes are separate and sequential. What's implied by this is that Sales & Marketing puts together a forecast and hands it off to Operations, who puts together a production plan which is sent directly into Master Production Scheduling.

Figure D-2, depicting Sales & Operations Planning, looks quite different. It shows both the sales planning function and the operations planning function occurring jointly, not sequentially. It indicates that there is interaction between the Sales Plan and Operations Plan, which of course is what I've been presenting throughout this book.

The result of the cross-functional Sales & Operations Planning process is the companywide game plan for Sales & Marketing, Operations, Finance, and Product Development — far more than a production plan.

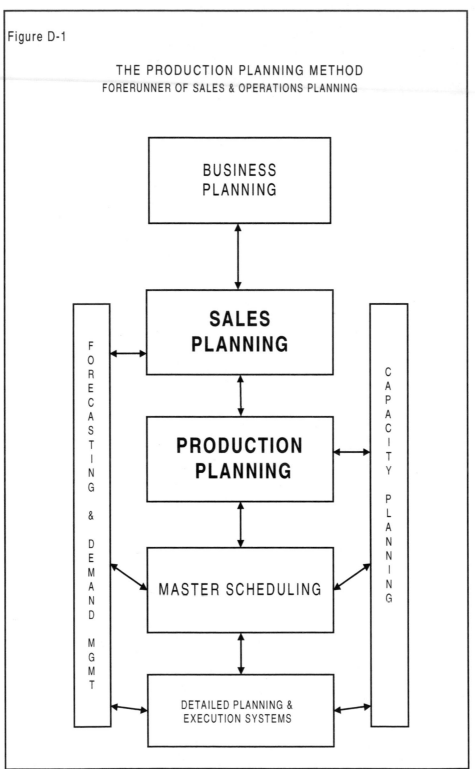

Figure D-1

THE PRODUCTION PLANNING METHOD
FORERUNNER OF SALES & OPERATIONS PLANNING

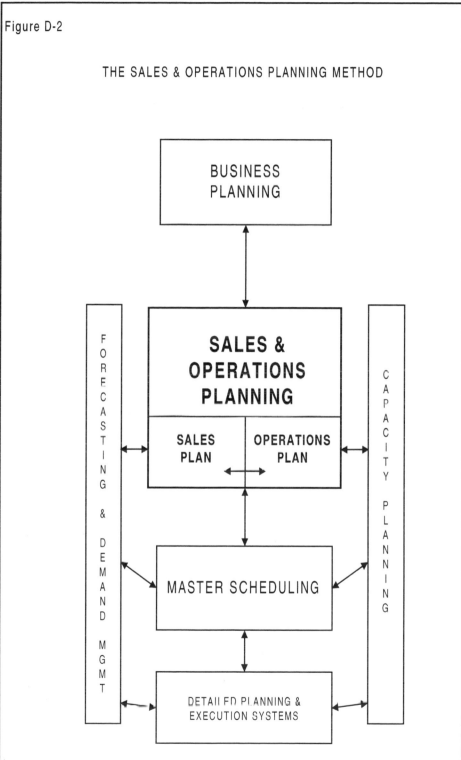

Figure D-2

THE SALES & OPERATIONS PLANNING METHOD

Index